T0352983

Repairing Play

Playful Thinking

Jesper Juul, Geoffrey Long, William Uricchio, and Mia Consalvo, editors

Repairing Play

A Black Phenomenology

Aaron Trammell

The MIT Press

Cambridge, Massachusetts | London, England

The MIT Press would like to thank the anonymous peer reviewers who provided comments on drafts of this book. The generous work of academic experts is essential for establishing the authority and quality of our publications. We acknowledge with gratitude the contributions of these otherwise uncredited readers.

This book was set in ITC Stone Serif Std and ITC Stone Sans Std by New Best-set Typesetters Ltd. Printed and bound in the United States of America.

Library of Congress Cataloging-in-Publication Data

Names: Trammell, Aaron, author.
Title: Repairing play : a Black phenomenology / Aaron Trammell.
Description: Cambridge, Massachusetts : The MIT Press, [2023] |
    Series: Playful thinking | Includes bibliographical references and
    index.
Identifiers: LCCN 2022013946 (print) | LCCN 2022013947 (ebook) |
    ISBN 9780262545273 (paperback) | ISBN 9780262373876 (epub) |
    ISBN 9780262373883 (pdf)
Subjects: LCSH: Play—Social aspects. | African Americans—
    Recreation. | African Americans—Social conditions. |
    Phenomenological sociology.
Classification: LCC GV14.45 .T73 2023 (print) | LCC GV14.45
    (ebook) | DDC 306.4/810973—dc23/eng/20220624
LC record available at https://lccn.loc.gov/2022013946
LC ebook record available at https://lccn.loc.gov/2022013947

10 9 8 7 6 5 4 3 2 1

Contents

On Thinking Playfully

Many people (we series editors included) find video games exhilarating, but it can be just as interesting to ponder why that is so. What do video games do? What can they be used for? How do they work? How do they relate to the rest of the world? Why is play both so important and so powerful?

Playful Thinking is a series of short, readable, and argumentative books that share some playfulness and excitement with the games that they are about. Each book in the series is small enough to fit in a backpack or coat pocket, and combines depth with readability for any reader interested in playing more thoughtfully or thinking more playfully. This includes, but is by no means limited to, academics, game makers, and curious players.

So, we are casting our net wide. Each book in our series provides a blend of new insights and interesting arguments with overviews of knowledge from game studies and other areas. You will see this reflected not just in the range of titles in our series but also in the range of authors creating them. Our basic assumption is simple: video games are such a flourishing medium that any new perspective on them is likely to show us something unseen or forgotten, including those from such unconventional voices as artists, philosophers, or specialists in other industries or fields of study. These books are bridge builders, cross-pollinating both areas with new knowledge and new ways of thinking.

At its heart, this is what Playful Thinking is all about: new ways of thinking about games and new ways of using games to think about the rest of the world.

Jesper Juul
Geoffrey Long
William Uricchio
Mia Consalvo

Acknowledgments

I would like to thank everybody who has supported me intellectually, spiritually, and creatively, during my time writing this book. I hope that this book gives back to the world a fraction of the joy, energy, support, and care that you have given to me this past year.

First, I would like to thank my father, who taught me what it means to be Black; my mother, who has always reminded me of the joys of creativity; and my sister, with whom I share the same complexity of identity and childhood experience. I dedicate this book to my family—mixed and beautiful—for encouraging me to explore the intersection of play and race. I love and understand you all more than you will ever know.

I could not have written this book without the support of my scholarly community either. Thank you to Kristine Jørgensen, Riccardo Fassone, Tom Apperley, and Kishonna Gray for reviewing and offering superlative feedback on the essay that this book developed out of, "Torture, Play, and the Black Experience"; your insights helped shape the book you hold before you today. Additionally, thank you Mia Consalvo, Geoffrey Long, Jesper Juul, and William Uricchio for reviewing the preliminary manuscript with such a generous eye to detail. Shira Chess, Souvik Mukherjee, Soraya Murray, Chris Paul, Nick Taylor, Adrienne Shaw, Sara Stang, Peter McDonald, Steven Dashiell, Alenda Chang, Thiago Falcao, Alexander Carneiro, Eddo Sterne, John Sharp, Sam Tobin, James Hodges, Robby Ratan, Cynthia Wang, and Lindsay Grace, thank you for all of the amazing conversations, encouragement, and support. I appreciate also the work of this book's anonymous reviewers, as well as the tireless effort that the MIT Press's Noah Springer and Lillian Dunaj have put into supporting the book through the publishing process. From the bottom of my heart, thank you.

The previous list only scratches the surface. I couldn't have written this without the support of my community here at the University of California Irvine (UCI). Roderic Crooks, Bo Ruberg, Katie Salen-Tekinbaş, and Braxton Soderman, I cannot tell you how invaluable your feedback on this project has been. Support cannot be limited to feedback, and so I also must thank my excellent colleagues Sameer Singh, Tess Tanenbaum, Karen Tanenbaum, Daniel Epstein, Elena Agapie, David Redmiles, Paul Dourish, Melissa Mazmanian, and Kylie Peppler for helping to provide a healthy community where I could thrive while completing this work. This extends also to the present and past graduate student community at UCI as well: Amanda Cullen, Forest Scully-Blaker, Ke Jing, Ian Larson, Kat Brewster, William Dunkel, Spencer Ruelos, Justin Keever, Izzy Williams, Bryan Truitt, Brandon Blackburn, Adrianna Burton, Dan Gardner, Emory Edwards, Kate Ringland, Bono Olgado, and Nikki Crenshaw, your encouragement and support has meant more to me than you will ever know.

I am also indebted to the intellectual support from the *Analog Game Studies* and *Sounding Out!* publishing communities. Evan Torner, Shelly Jones, Megan Condis, Liana Silva and Edmond Chang thank you for being such amazing and supportive colleagues. Jenny Stoever, thank you for always believing in me. The material in this book goes all the way back to your Popular Music and Representation class—I hope I have treated it with a fraction of the integrity that you have in your research, teaching, and everyday practice. Likewise, I am indebted to the band Bad Brains, who let me reprint the excellent lyrics to "Pay to Cum" free of charge. You are the real deal. Thank you!

Paul Greenleaf and Lizzie Stark, you have my heart and gratitude for reading and reviewing an early version of this manuscript. Thank you for caring for and cultivating my tender and tentative early writing. Of course, I owe Andrew Schrock a word of thanks too. Your support and engagement with my writing have made all the difference, and I could not have done this without you.

Thank you Suesan Cota, Colin Germain, Katie Germain, Dan Ubinski, and Lana Sacks for always being down to talk things through, your friendship means everything to me, and I couldn't have written this without your support. Finally, I need to thank my love Emma for always listening, always reading, and for supporting me through the long and difficult process of writing. I could not have written this without you.

Introduction

All day long they work so hard till the sun is goin' down
Working on the highways and byways and wearin' a
frown
Hear them moanin' their lives away
Then you hear somebody say
That's the sound of the men working on the chain gang.
—"Chain Gang," written by Sam Cooke*

Let's start with the problem: our definition of play is broken. We game scholars know this intimately because we have watched as the term's emancipatory potentials were appropriated and co-opted by hatred, far-right rhetoric, and bigotry over the last decade. One need go no further than a game's voice chat, Twitch stream, or Reddit forum to observe how neatly adolescent hate speech sits alongside gameplay. Was Gamergate the

---

*Published by ABKCO Music, Inc. All rights reserved. Used with permission.

moment when play was appropriated by hate? Or was it instead the moment when a century of rot eating away at the concept finally broke through? Folks, our ship is sinking, and we're about to be washed out to sea. Maybe we've been on this ship so long that we've forgotten what freedom is. Is play our savior or our oppressor?

Pause. Let me take a beat to define play. Most people picking up this book already have some mental model of the term. There are a few typical characteristics that are common to most definitions of play. Here are the basics: play is fun, and it's often pleasurable; play is universal, interspecies even; it is consensual or voluntary; and, finally, play is a behavior; it's something you *do*. There is more to it, of course, but for most folks the previous definition will suffice. In this book, I argue that this definition of play is only half-baked. I share how this definition might alienate Black, Indigenous, and People of Color (BIPOC) from spaces of play that were previously viewed as inclusive. Moreover, I want to convince you that an inclusive, and thus reparative, definition of play is as painful as it is pleasurable, as individual as it is universal, and as mandatory as it is voluntary. If this interests you, by all means, read on.

The Black radical tradition is filled with stories of slave ships. It's also replete with tales of art, music, and other forms of play that have little to do with games. "That's the sound of the men working on the chain gang," goes the refrain of an old Sam Cooke song. The men in the song are singing, but they're also in pain.

They're singing about how agonizing their work is and how miserable they are. The singing itself gives them hope. *They're playing.* Play as read through the lens of the Black radical tradition is about diving into the messiness of life, seeking a philosophical praxis that is down, around, outside, and always just out of reach. The slave ship defines the Black radical tradition, just as its specter haunts all of us who think within it. It's a history of dislocation, relocation, trauma, pain, and suffering. It's a hideous legacy, for sure. But it inadvertently produced kinship between centuries of Black folk slowly piecing back together what centuries of colonialism broke.

Fred Moten and Stefano Harney unflinchingly define Blackness as, "the site where absolute nothingness and the world of things converge. Blackness is fantasy in the hold. . . . We are the shipped, if we choose to be, if we elect to pay an unbearable cost that is inseparable from an incalculable benefit" (Harney and Moten 2013, 95). Black folk share a traumatic history that has its roots in the slave trade. We are "the shipped" because we have been imprisoned in the cargo holds of slave ships and treated as objects. Black subjectivity in this tradition thus inhabits objectification while contending with a colonized past and the possibility of a shackled future. In other words, being Black is just as much about skin tone as it is about history. As a people, we now will forever contend with a history of murder, rape, abuse, appropriation, and enslavement. We have been treated like objects, bought and sold in markets, stuffed alongside inanimate goods on slave ships. Yet we embrace this history; it is through resilience that we are united. Despite the pain, we memorialize and share the traumas of the slave trade—and therefore the horrors of colonialism—with one another. The discomfort of living in this place and embodying this history is itself the potential of the Black radical tradition. Embracing and understanding this dissonant place is reparative. I locate within it a common ethic of resistance, struggle, and even survival.

I invoke the history of Black folk abducted on slave ships because this book specifically argues that torture—as a trauma passed down from one generation to the next—is an important part of the Black experience in North America. An experience that unfortunately resonates with countless other BIPOC globally who themselves have been abused, tortured, and worse by slavers, merchants, and governments. From these shared legacies of abuse, we find solidarity. I want to be explicit that I do not feel that being descended from slaves is either an essential part of the BIPOC experience in North America or globally.[1] Yet this tradition is the one I was raised within, and so I feel driven to speak to it as a way to reconsider a definition of play.[2]

But what do slave ships have to do with play? In short, this book is an attempt to repair a definition of play that has been largely informed by scholars and philosophers working within a White, European tradition. This tradition of play, theorized most famously by Dutch historian Johan Huizinga, French sociologist Roger Caillois, and Swiss psychologist Jean Piaget, reads play in a mostly positive sense. They assert that certain practices—namely, torture—are taboo and thus cannot be play. I argue that this approach to play is shortsighted and linked to a troubling global discourse that renders the experiences of BIPOC invisible. In other words, by defining play only through its pleasurable connotations, the term holds a bias toward people with access to the conditions of leisure. Indeed, torture helps paint a more complete picture of play, in which its most heinous potentials are addressed alongside the most pleasant. In so doing, the trauma of slavery is remembered and re-embedded in the very concept of play. In rethinking the phenomenology of play, I will detail the more insidious ways that play has functioned as a tool of subjugation. A tool that hurts as much as it heals and has been complicit in the systemic erasure of BIPOC people from the domain of leisure.

There is an urgent social imperative for this work. The Black Lives Matter protests that unfolded globally in the summer of 2020 spoke explicitly about how the erasure of BIPOC people from White social spaces in North America through the threat of torture and violence continues to subjugate entire communities. Practices that divide and exclude only exacerbate the problem of racist exclusion. For this reason, I argue that it is crucial to rethink the politics of play in our present moment. Approaches that misconstrue play as an innately good or positive activity run afoul of this problematic. They ultimately intone that those with access to leisure time engage in activities that are generally positive, constructive, and wholesome. We must urgently rethink the very definition of play to make space for those it has oppressed, as well as those it has elevated. By rethinking play, we might recognize how the alibi it provides has enabled toxic communities to thrive. After all, Gamergate, the "alt-right," steroid use in sports, and hazing rituals all owe something to play as well. The tradition of Black people descended from slaves specifically shows how we might use these tragic moments of play to create a more inclusive and reparative definition of the term.

The road toward a more inclusive study of play has been a bumpy one. Toward this end, I find it useful to disambiguate studies of games from the study of play. Game studies considers games as objects and play studies theorizes play as an embodied practice. Game studies is a younger area of scholarship that draws on many canonical theories of play. It places an emphasis on both the narrative and mechanical structures that constitute games. Thus, game studies is interested in what games are, who plays games, and the social impacts of games. Although game studies scholarship often draws upon studies of play, it is generally more engaged with theorizing games themselves. In comparison to work in game studies, work in what I call play theory has a relatively longer arc. Play theory generally considers play as an activity. Game studies scholars might consider a game that is never played, and likewise, play theorists might consider forms of play that exist outside of games.

Unlike play theory, game studies has been wrestling with questions of inclusivity for at least two decades. I concur with Kishonna Gray's assessment that "a focus should be placed on how technology is mobilized to fulfill the project of White masculine supremacy" (Gray 2020, 4). Like many other game studies scholars, Gray implicitly theorizes technology through the medium of computer games. Computer games show how people navigate technology (both computers and software) in everyday life. And because people talk about their experiences playing games, they offer researchers insight into the subjective experience of technology. As such, games allow players to flirt with the pleasurable aspects of White supremacy by granting them the agency to engage in what Lisa Nakamura terms "identity tourism" (Nakamura 2005, para. 8) and what David Leonard considers "digital minstrelsy" (Leonard 2006, 87). For these scholars—and others like Jennifer Malkowski and TreaAndrea M. Russworm (2017, 3) who see an immediate and direct correlation between the textual content of games and the everyday politics of gamers —representation matters. But what if these theorizations that address inclusivity as a problem of gamers, games, and gaming are too specific? This book considers how these insights from an intersectional analysis of games and gamers might be applied to the very practice of play.

The problem of inclusivity in games that the afore-mentioned scholarship engages with is symptomatic of a larger problem in play studies. In order to address the problem of inclusivity in play studies, this book will confront yet another taboo—it will attempt to challenge and decolonize White European thought through the theory and language used in White European critical theory. I admire how the work of theorists like Samantha Blackmon and TreaAndrea M. Russworm uses the language of the "mix tape" to recenter Black women in a narrative around games that seeks to decenter their importance (Russworm and Blackmon 2020, 99). They organize their writing musically, splicing in lyrics by Black women to help tell the same story a different way. The idea is to show how the knowledge produced by folk in the community is a form of scholarship that is at least the equivalent of the traditional academic essay.

I dig this approach. It has been highly influential to my own thinking on the topic. In this book, I talk about music and weave song lyrics performed by Black artists into the text to drive home the point that a good deal of this material has been discussed by Black folk already—even if it's formalization as an academic argument is itself novel. I admire the way Blackmon and Russworm make space for Black scholars to talk about play in their own voice. It's essential to have spaces where we don't have to code switch—a point I will return to in chapter 1 when I discuss the jargon of crows. Some readers will doubtlessly find some passages in this book curious, cryptic, and wildering. This is deliberate. I mean to challenge the norms of White European scholarship with my writing. Accordingly, I vary my approach in this book by toggling between the language and methods of critical race studies and theoretical conjectures more common in the canon of White European play studies. Throughout, I focus specifically on amending the work taken up by a lineage of White European theory that has historically excluded BIPOC folk. In this sense, *Repairing Play* gives life to a form of play that attends to the traumatic aspects of play and serves as a form of reparations. After almost a century of colonizing play that centers a White European perspective, we must totally rethink the premises upon which this theory is predicated.

At the heart of my argument lies the premise that theories of play see it as a constructive and positive form of leisure. Accordingly, we must work to reconcile these theorizations with the fact that play is often hurtful, toxic, and haphazard. Historically, this theorizing has taken place in several domains. Johan Huizinga (1980) neglects gambling in the entirety of 1938's *Homo Ludens* because of its associations with the amoral connotations that were associated with the activity at the time.[3] Roger Caillois (2001), writing in 1961, uses the term "corruption" to discuss forms of play that he finds troubling or unpalatable.[4] Jean Piaget (1962) and Lev Vygotsky's ([1966] 2015) respective theories of play—and the educational theory of constructivism that follows[5]—are predicated on the idea that play is the mechanism that structures learning. These ideas have been tremendously important in game studies as well. Katie Salen and Eric Zimmerman's influential reading of Huizinga's magic circle (2003) has been so often uncritically cited as a way to explain games as a positive activity that it prompted Zimmerman to clarify his position in an op-ed for *Gamasutra* entitled, "Jerked Around by the Magic Circle" (Zimmerman 2012). Scholarship on games and learning; serious games; and games and literacy builds on Piaget and Vygotsky's theory of play and cognition. But play is not always constructive; it can also be oppressive and traumatic.

Theorists have attempted to reconcile the creative and destructive aspects of play. Brian Sutton-Smith argues (1997) that "play" holds a variety of valences and can thus be used to achieve a variety of rhetorical ends. He argues that play is often used to advance a perspective that assumes playfulness relates to progress (learning through play), fate (play of chance), power (the play of sport and contest), identity (rituals of group identity), the imaginary (play and creativity), the self (playful hobbies that result in individuation), or frivolousness (play as an idle, leisurely activity; Sutton-Smith 1997, 8–11). In approaching play through a rhetorical lens, however, Smith treats all of these rhetorics as equal in impact. I deviate from Smith in this book, as I feel that the basic phenomenology of play is a power relationship. The moment people engage in what Judith Butler (1990, xxxiii) terms an "activity play," they are conjuring this relationship. As this book will detail in chapter 3, this performative act has an uneasy and violent grammar that casts the player as a subject, and the game and its other players as objects. A radical phenomenology of play centers on the moments when play is painful (as opposed to pleasurable) to recenter the BIPOC narratives that focus on the traumatic and violent aspects of games and play.

The trauma of slavery in North America is not only remembered through storytelling; it is also memorialized in forms of play. Among the most mythic and controversial games that young Black children played in the postbellum (post–Civil War) United States was "Hide the Switch." In this game, players would root around for a hidden switch, and once found, the finder was granted free rein to flog the other players, who attempted to parry the attack. Historians considering the game's persistence within slave culture have been challenged by it because the game reinforces the martial conditions of bondage. Many explanations have been offered to explain its endurance, often as a form of "coping." Some historians suggest that the game allowed children to practice avoiding punishment. Others believe that the game allowed enslaved Black children a brief moment of liberation by allowing them to role-play being the "master" (King 2011, 117–8). Both explanations are ultimately uncomfortable, as they attempt to reconcile the violence of the experience of Black folk descended from slaves by drawing on the inevitable lighthearted connotations of play. Historians thus perpetuate a trend in which torture is either reduced to a carnivalesque inversion of power dynamics—where the victim becomes the oppressor—or violence is reduced to discipline—a tactic for living within its inevitability.

A good deal of my writing in this book deals with what I and several other scholars working in a wide array of fields term "affect." Affect is a tricky word to define because its definition varies greatly between fields. Where a cognitive psychologist might measure affect with sensors that track the beads of sweat secreted by a television viewer, a literary theorist might consider the emotions and moods experienced in the shadow of monuments. Simply defined, affect can be read as stimulus and response. But, in practice, the terms are used in a way that hints at far more—in sum, affect is a way of signaling the investigation of the minute and difficult to perceive connections that exist between all things.

I should also take a moment to discuss what I mean by torture. I situate my understanding of torture within the tradition established by the philosopher Michel Foucault. As a practice, torture is a long-term form of discipline that uses coercive techniques to subjugate people. Torture runs the gamut from its most brutal forms—waterboarding, for example—to playground bullying, to its most pleasurable extreme—BDSM. I argue in this book that it is a mistake to view "tickle torture" and BDSM as merely "innocent" forms of torture. For even in the most innocent and pleasurable acts of play, we subtly discipline those around us to engage in unspoken rules. Relatedly, I define pleasure in an affective sense; pleasure drives desire and is often juxtaposed against pain, another affect. Torture and play are both practices that produce affects of pleasure or pain.

In this book, I am concerned with brutal, disciplinary, and militaristic torture because I feel they are undertheorized and seen as taboo in the study of games and play. The relationship between torture and pleasure, on the other hand, has been better theorized in work that analyzes social practices within BDSM communities worldwide. J. Tuomas Harviainen's (2011) work shows how BDSM might be considered play. Yet it and other similar analyses stop short of including military and disciplinary torture (Weiss 2011, 211). This is because they theorize BDSM mainly as a form of consensual play. Instead, this book argues that we must understand military and disciplinary torture—with its connotations of pain and not pleasure (and not pleasurable pain)—as play. What's more, I advocate for a definition of play that overcomes what I see as a fundamental taboo: play is allowed to be pleasurable but not torturous. Yet so much of play *is* torturous: BDSM, memorizing long lists of rules, exhausting one's physical limits, and the tedium of simply playing Monopoly. This seeming paradox—that torture both is and is not play—can be resolved. Torture *is* play, and approaching it as such reveals a good deal about how play subjugates and disciplines people.

Although this book looks at torture as a specific form of play, I implore my readers to consider a wide gamut of ways that they may have encountered painful moments of play in their own lives. This occurs all the time in the schoolyard. Children hound, chase, and tease one another mercilessly. What is often common sense for a six-year-old—that the playground can be a scary and unruly place—is seen by the aforementioned canon of play theorists through the overtly racist lens of "savage" play. I argue that bullying, too, is a form of play. We all have experienced play's dark and troubling proclivities. Definitions of play that ignore these aspects of play exclude through omission anesthetize the concept, thus offering what I feel is an incomplete theory of play.

Recognizing how play is often experienced as torture might also help us better understand how the application of the term has been historically used to exclude BIPOC, women, trans people, and nonbinary folk from historically White and masculine spaces of play.[6] When play is only theorized as pleasure, minoritized[7] people are made to act as "killjoys" when they describe their play experiences as torturous.[8] The concept this book puts forth—*repairing play*—is meant to open the concept of play up in a way that is more inclusive. It means contending both with how play includes (through pleasure) and how play excludes (through torture). Repairing play is simultaneously a form of intellectual reparations that amends the commonsense notion that play is pleasurable and a form of play that focuses on exploring the deep, painful, and sometimes traumatic depths of life.

The discomfort I noted previously when describing "Hide the Switch" relates to the relationship between play and cultural identity. This game predominantly existed within an oral history of slavery passed down through generations of Black folk. It is best pondered as an artifact of a bygone era that is better left in the past. Still, we can recognize the social repression of "Hide the Switch" as a process through which the dynamics of play were culturally controlled and regulated. Similar to the hypervigilant policing of Black people in early twenty-first-century America, Black children's games have also been repressed and policed. Small and invisible, the historical policing of play has contributed to the cultural erasure of BIPOC today. Thus in play, because the brutality of slavery cannot be shared, we are left with a concept that relates to torture only in so far as it is pleasurable. In other words, a Black phenomenology of play begins with the notion that torture is a form of play.

To explore this argument, this book is divided into five chapters and a conclusion. It begins by revealing how the definitions of play popularized by White European philosophers are predicated on a racist binary. I look at the work of Johan Huizinga, Roger Caillois, Jean

Piaget, and other canonical theorists of play theory to demonstrate how many canonical definitions of play presume that play is productive of "civilization." This conceit—however useful it may be for those who might advocate for play's virtues as a tool of education and training—is fundamentally White supremacist. In the first chapter, "Decolonizing Play," I work through the reasons that early play theory argues that play is productive and explain how the presumed opposite of "civilization," barbarism, is often invoked to dehumanize and disparage BIPOC people. I argue that this distinction produces a double standard between the painful and pleasurable potentials of play. The painful potentials of play are quarantined, set apart from the pleasurable play that "civilized" people enjoy.

If play is not productive of "civilization," what does it produce? The second chapter of this book, "Play as Affect," argues that play is productive of affect. The affects of civility that the theorists in the first chapter lauded so keenly are most closely affiliated with the pleasurable. The affects most verboten in these texts are associated most with the traumatic and painful. By focusing on the pleasurable as opposed to the painful, theories of play exclude BIPOC people through erasure. Games like "Hide the Switch" noted earlier become arcane riddles of play that are only accessible through history books—"barbaric" stereotypes of how wild children play when raised outside of White European culture. *Repairing Play* is a phenomenology of play that begins with the painful and traumatic affects that are produced by play to develop a definition that better speaks to the lived experiences of BIPOC people. But if play is productive of painful affects, we must also contend with the question of how central consent is to repairing play.

The third chapter of this book, "Play as Capture," imagines the White European grammar of play through the language of law enforcement. It asks readers to wrestle with whether their captivation with play is actually a form of capture or arrest. Here I reject readings of play that treat it as morally ambiguous. A reparative definition of play must contend with the term's ultimate ambivalence by returning to how play's vertiginous potentials, madness, violence, disorder, and dissonance help close the phenomenological loop. Indeed, play will remain complicit in the erasure of BIPOC people until we contend with the disturbing and grotesque ways that people have been toyed with, tortured, and made to endure horrors in the name of play.

"Torture and the Black American Experience" is the fourth chapter of this book. It explores the historical relationship between torture and the experience of Black people descended from slavery. I draw on the history of Black people in North America specifically because it is one of many BIPOC histories that centralizes torture in its narrative and can thus speak to both the pleasurable and painful dynamics of play. Additionally, it is the story I know best because I have grown up within this tradition. The chapter uses slave songs as an example of how play communicates the pain of abuse and serves as a way to cope with and produce a spirituality around the collective suffering endured by Black Americans. These perspectives on torture help us better comprehend play's fuller dimensions and how it might resuscitate a phenomenology of play today.

The arc of this book ends with the fifth chapter, "Recentering Blackness in Games and Play." The goal of this final chapter is to draw on examples of Black play from a variety of media to show the stories that a repaired play might allow to be told. From theater, to video games, to marbles, I endeavor to offer examples of Black art that challenge the European definition of play that has haunted the entirety of this book. Through these examples, I hope to show the reader how this project of repairing play has long been the lifework of Black artists. Play has been complicit in the erasure of BIPOC people insofar as our work, energy, and creativity have been belittled and read as tangential to the main creative products that are marketed through play. We cannot believe in the dream of a repaired play until we see that BIPOC people have been dreaming it all along.

Finally, the book ends where it began, concluding with "Repairing Play." *Repairing Play* is both a play on reparations—the financial compensation sought by Black people from the state for centuries of bondage— and the idea that a new form of play that is inclusive of BIPOC people may be reparative. By insisting on a radical new practice of play that memorializes its most harmful abuses, we can envision a more thoughtful kind of playing where players are aware of the potential violence that lurks in an unlikely roll of dice.

To repair play, we must strip away the racist dichotomies of civilization and barbarism that were used to justify the slave trade. We must abandon the conceit that some forms of play are more intellectual or noble than others. For until we do, we are all in the hold together on a sinking ship in dire need of repair. Here in the hold, there is an ember of hope. As critical race theorist Frank Wilderson has written, "I would make my home in the hold of the ship and burn it from the inside out" (Wilderson 2020, 323). Indeed, let the blaze of the slave ship cast our shadows over the inferno of play that colonizes everything it touches. This play that is rooted in a fundamental and toxic lie of equity, morality, education, and leisure has long excluded BIPOC people—but we know how to repair it. And we shall dance, sing, chant, and celebrate as we do.

1

Decolonizing Play

Southern trees bear a strange fruit
Blood on the leaves and blood at the root
Black bodies swingin' in the Southern breeze
Strange fruit hangin' from the poplar trees
Pastoral scene of the gallant South
The bulgin' eyes and the twisted mouth
Scent of magnolias sweet and fresh
Then the sudden smell of burnin' flesh
Here is a fruit for the crows to pluck
For the rain to gather
For the wind to suck
For the sun to rot
For the tree to drop
Here is a strange and bitter crop
　　　　　　　—Billie Holiday, "Strange Fruit," 1939*

---

*First published as the poem "Bitter Fruit" by Abel Meeropol in 1937.

Crows play. Researchers who observe their behavior have found seven main practices that resemble what philosophers call "play." Crows manipulate objects for no apparent reason, hide things, and perform tricks while flying. They mess around with water while bathing, slide down slopes, vocalize aimlessly, and hang on branches upside down (Heinrich and Smolker 1998). But the crows in the epigraph ain't playing—they're surviving. Billy Holiday's *Strange Fruit* is a protest song. It's a graphic description of the lynchings Black folk suffered in America throughout its history. And while the tune may have changed—the hangman's noose today is less popular than the pistol and the police no longer wear hoods—the song remains the same. Black people in the United States and Black, Indigenous, and People of Color (BIPOC) people across the world are more likely to be killed by the authorities, their neighbors, or complete strangers than their White counterparts. This is the rationale for the Black Lives Matter movement, and an upsetting reminder of how unjust and inequitable society remains. To repair play, we must first recognize how deeply indebted the concept of play is to White European thought and consider how this lineage has created significant blind spots in our discourse of play. Most notably, play theory insists on elevating play to a virtue—an art of modern progress—and characterizes the forms of play that compete with this narrative as corrupt. They are not "true" play.

Before digging into the canon of play theory, let's return to crows for a second. These scavengers might be more helpful in addressing the problem of play than one might initially think. Although animals play, their play is unproductive. The canon of play theory derived from the work of Johan Huizinga (1980) makes a crucial, influential argument that left an indelible mark on a good deal of research that has followed: play itself is productive of civilization. He writes, "Now in myth and ritual the great instinctive forces of civilized life have their origin: law and order, commerce and profit, craft and art, poetry, wisdom and science. All are rooted in the primaeval soil of play" (Huizinga 1980, 5). He implies that "civilized" is all that is legible to Western European "civilization." The opposite, as I will catalogue here, is barbarism. Likewise, he implies that the civilized is that which is human, while the barbaric is that which is not. Thus, he assumes that people whose customs are not legible to Western Civilization act much like animals. They are like the crows, trifling with baubles with no particular goal or end in mind. For the presumably "civilized," play is always constructive of something.

Billie Holiday once sang of crows. "Strange Fruit" was a song about how the presumably "civilized" White folk in America, were themselves barbaric. The crows in the song bore witness to the murder. They know that from the perspective of countless BIPOC folk globally, the arbiters of "civilization" themselves, the police, are barbaric. To underscore the point, police *do* play. They play with guns, they play in uniforms, and they perform authority as they toy with the folks they encounter on the beat. Contemporary social movements like All Cops Are Bastards spell this out by showing how the police are, in so many instances, guilty of transgressing the very laws that they are sworn to uphold. Recognizing the barbarism at the core of "civilization" is core to the Black experience in North America. We have all had "the talk" about how to behave when pulled over. We know, just as the crows do, that the project of "civilization" is itself the project of White supremacy.

The problem with "civilized" play, as I describe it in this chapter, is that it pits BIPOC people against each other. The Disney film *Dumbo* speaks volumes. In *Dumbo*, the eponymous protagonist elephant is antagonized and later befriended by a murder of crows. The crows are illustrated as "hep-cats" speaking in jive and singing scat—and of course, they're Black. In the original release of *Dumbo*, the main crow was named Jim Crow—an allusion to the offensive minstrel performer who used that moniker in the nineteenth century. The racism in the movie is so blatant that Disney later changed the character's name to Dandy Crow in an effort to make the movie less obviously offensive. The crows in the film are playful—they sing, cackle, and strut around. This scene shows how the play of Black people was appropriated, twisted, and commodified by a White film studio. Yet this inclusion was defended by

Floyd Norman, the first Black man hired as an animator by Disney.

In defense of the crows, Norman invokes the naive gaiety of "fun" as a rationale. He wrote an article for his blog entitled "Black Crows and Other PC Nonsense," in which he explains, "If you remember the story, a group of cool crows nesting in a field decide to have some fun at the elephant's expense. After Timothy Mouse scolds the feathered group, they soon have a change of heart and decide to encourage the little elephant. The song they sing is pure fun and entertainment and the animation is inspired."[1] Norman's opinion is clearly colored by the unique pressures he faced as the first Black animator hired by Disney. Many "model minorities"— particularly the first BIPOC people in their industry— feel a pressure to perform not just competency at their craft but also cultural competency with the social norms of the community that they enter. Norman defends the inclusion of Black characters in *Dumbo*, despite the stereotypes they embody, at the expense of critiquing the White supremacist culture from which they had been created. If Norman were to call the crows out as racist, he would be seen as critiquing the company (and thus his peers) as racists. He would violate a social norm and risk being seen as uncivilized. In other words, he would be playing the spoilsport.

Leisure, fun, and games are all pathologies of an understanding of play that ignores the traumatic and painful aspects of play, instead making it—by definition

—something positive. But experiencing play and civilization as pleasures is a privilege that is at odds with the lived experiences of BIPOC people. "Civilization" has disciplined BIPOC people for centuries, it is the colonial force that put a boot to our necks, stole our land, and enslaved us. If play is productive of civilization, then by extension play must have had a hand in the evils of colonization. To read play as mere leisure is a privilege, a privilege afforded to White people. This is why stereotypes of Black people goofing off, having fun, and hanging out are read so negatively—leisure is part of White privilege. A Black man at a country club? He's going to be watched closely by security. I've had to turn over my bags at game shops and comic book stores as dubious clerks cased and profiled me.

When they aren't depicted as animals, the Black men in *Dumbo* are hard at work. The "jive crows" are contrasted with a Black chain gang (called the Roustabouts) elsewhere in the movie. The Roustabouts are depicted as lazy and drink, smoke, and play instead of work. Particularly offensive are the ways that the Roustabouts sing that their work is "happy," while swinging heavy hammers. On all levels, the message is clear: If you're Black you better wear a smile and be "happy" no matter how painful or traumatic your work is. You're going to be seen as lazy no matter what, and you sure don't get to say what counts as fun.

So how did we come to agree upon a canon of play theory that colludes so readily with the ideology of

White supremacy? This question, in my opinion, is philosophical in nature. It asks us to review theories about what play is—in other words, research that has been done on the phenomenology of play. Phenomenology is a domain of study that offers a scientific and cultural account of how practices, play for instance, are structured. It asks questions about why several experiences of the same thing, or "phenomenon," differ from one another? Because I argue that repairing play means understanding how play is experienced differently by BIPOC people, the argument is phenomenological in scope. So is the canonical argument made by Johan Huizinga. Huizinga argues that by playing, we make society, or more specifically, "civilization." His theory suggests that there is a structure to both "civilization" and play and that these two structures are linked. As I discuss later in this chapter, the problem with Huizinga's argument is that his definition of "civilization" is almost exclusively a White European one. It is less an argument about what happens when people play and instead a phenomenological argument about what happens when White people play.

Because Huizinga only accounts for European "civilization" in his writing, his account of play is naive. It renders both play and "civilization" in mostly positive terms, and thus sidesteps the abuses, traumas, and pain that play connotes for BIPOC people. Margaret Carlisle Duncan, in her close reading of *Homo Ludens*, notes this exactly. She explains the contradictions of Huizinga and argues, "Play scholars have failed in their attempts to conceptualize play *precisely because they have ignored the ideological dimensions of their subject* which lie not in play but in discourse (i.e., reflection and talk) about play" (Duncan 1988, 29). Otherwise stated, play theorists have a tendency to read play as phenomenology, not ideology. I concur with Duncan's larger point, to assume that play exists outside of discourse, and thus ideology, is a romantic and dangerous notion. As we know well today, play is political, and approaches to the topic further the dynamics of White supremacy when they are naive to the implications that play is a form of power. Repairing play deliberately centers BIPOC people for this reason. Challenging ideology means offering alternatives to it and drawing on histories and experiences of the invisible, exploited, and otherwise abused.

Duncan advocates that we understand the rhetoric of play precisely so that we can critique its ideological character. Yet this solution sits uncomfortably with me as I read it in the aftermath of the radicalization of far-right politics in 2021. Gamergate, QAnon, and other avenues of radicalization today often use play as an alibi for aggressive, violent, and discriminatory behavior. Doing it "for the lulz" has become a callous expression of how the rhetoric of play as "free" is often used to defend the most egregious instances of play as violence. Thus, although I concur with Duncan that play is ideological, I find myself drawn to Huizinga's interest in the terms *phenomenological dimensions*. Because phenomenology considers the experience of inhabiting a body (Ahmed 2006, 544), I argue that Huizinga's mistake was simple: he didn't consult any BIPOC people about their experiences of play.

Thus, throughout this book, I argue that to repair play, we must center BIPOC people in the conversation. A Black phenomenology of play is both one of pain and pleasure. A recognition of how play can be painful would have resolved the contradictions that Huizinga himself fretted about while writing. Mathias Fuchs's historical work suggests that Huizinga's unpublished forward for *Homo Ludens* reveals a critical Huizinga concerned with how his theory of play may have appealed to the ideology of Nazi Germany as it "is often read in defense of 'free activity,' 'fixed rules,' and 'orderly manner'" (Fuchs 2014, 535). Even Huizinga, in reconsidering his own work after World War II, was aware of how the violent tendencies of play might complicate the potentials he would, unfortunately, term "civilized." Huizinga was watching the cops in Germany commit genocide. In returning to his own theories, he became troubled by their contradictions. If only he knew a few more Black folk, they would have told him that "civilization" ain't all it's cracked up to be.

It is pertinent then to reconsider play through a comparative approach that is critical of dominant theories. In 1938, Huizinga (1980), whose widely cited *Homo Ludens* has become a master text in the field of game studies, first approached play as a cultural phenomenon. The anthropological scholarship in his day approached rationality as an innate biological characteristic of "man." Huizinga hoped to disrupt this approach to what he termed the "human" by juxtaposing the "rational" society against the "playful" society.[2]

In Huizinga's definition, play is the preconscious act that is often labeled "ritual," "sacred," "natural." When unspoken (and therefore unlabeled) play manifests as a series of behavioral patterns common to both man and animal, listed as "order, tension, movement, change, solemnity, rhythm, rapture" (Huizinga 1980, 17). For Huizinga, there is a fundamental organizing function to play behavior. While efforts to explain it are often cast as ritual or myth, these labels are ultimately secondary. Because in Huizinga's work, play is the preconscious driver of ritual activity. Moments of play are fleeting and temporary, but there is a finite trace of play's significance in organizing the whole of Huizinga's imagined lifeworld.

Huizinga describes play as fundamental to a "later phase of society." This is a clear dog whistle for situating White European society as superior to BIPOC cultures that era anthropologists read as primitive. Although Huizinga takes steps to clarify that he feels cultures who primarily engage in ritual play might still be considered "man," it is worth noting that language that stratifies society into stages of development has been historically used as a way for White supremacist groups to argue for the virtues of "civilized" Western European culture. Although it is not clear how Huizinga disambiguated the crowing of colonized and indigenous people from the jargon of birds, he felt strongly that some social structures were more advanced than others. While Huizinga's approach is broad in its scope, at least one element of his argument still drives the dominant discourse: that play is a cultural (not biological) phenomenon. This differentiation is best seen in the work of Jean Piaget, a psychologist who argued the opposite.

Taking a psychological standpoint, Piaget (1962) considers play an intimate part of our physiological makeup.[3] While Piaget concurs with Huizinga's opinion that play is a preconscious act, he argues that it is biological in nature—a step in the development of our mental sensemaking organs.[4] The standpoint of cognitive psychology through which Piaget approaches his work is relevant insofar as it considers play a foundational psychological driver of rationality.[5] Piaget's theory of play presumes a type of rationality informed by the Western European enlightenment. This kind of rationality has historically excluded the cultures and practices of BIPOC people from the discourse of philosophical thought.

Where Huizinga took a broad approach to play and Piaget adopted a biologically essentialist perspective, Caillois analyzed play sociologically. Caillois (2001), who focuses specifically on the play of games, is somewhat critical of Huizinga and Piaget's work. He finds it curious that both omitted games of chance in their writings, and argues that this exclusion may relate to the audiences for which these scholars wrote. For Piaget, the moralistic connotations of gambling may have made its inclusion unpalatable to the educators interested in understanding play as a process of learning. As for Huizinga's omission, the inclusion of games of chance would threaten to undo his argument regarding the primacy of play as a civilizing cultural form. This would call into question those instances in which play is arguably at its most vertiginous. These are the moments in which gambling allows for individual transcendence of the economic order, like buying lotto tickets. These moments are also the most difficult to regulate and have found their strongest opponents in legal, and religious codes.

For Caillois (2001), White European society is explicitly the focus of play. He categorized Australian, American, and African aborigines "primitive societies" and referred to them as "Dionysian" contrasting them with the "rational" cultures of the Incas, Assyrians, Chinese, and Romans (87). Mimicry and vertigo, which he associates with "primitive" cultures and rituals, are said to corrupt competition and chance, which are associated with what Caillois (2001) saw as more sophisticated cultures. Competition and chance, of course, yield the meritocratic structures that underlie much of White European society. Importantly, it is vertigo that corrupts competition and mimicry which corrupts chance, not the other way around.[6] An anti-colonial approach to this problem might ask why it is that competition and chance are lauded in this instance, while mimicry and vertigo are decried? Caillois classifies these combinations as "forbidden play" and even maps them to cultures accordingly. His work speaks to the prejudice he brought to it, as he was concerned with miscegenation between different aspects of play.

Mihai Spariousu (1989) shows how deeply indebted thinking about play—as typified by Huizinga, Piaget, and Caillois—is to the canon of Western thought. In his book *Dionysus Reborn*, Spariousu compares approaches to play in the social sciences, philosophy, and literary theory. He locates a split in the Western consciousness along rational and prerational axes dating back to ancient Greece. Spariousu suggests that theory on the play concept has reflected this split.[7]

Games, for the most part, are theorized in all these contexts as rational, creative, ordered, and progressive extensions of play. Although games are often said to reflect the social order (Bowman 2010; Caillois 2001; Fine 2002; Hofer 2003), such a sentiment fails to question the racial politics of this social order. Indeed, any social order that reads the emotional against the rational has justified slavery and encouraged violence against women, nonbinary folks, and people of color in the name of "rationality." Spariousu's analysis, though uncritical of the cultural dynamics that take place within the social order produced by play, is spot on. We live in a society that denigrates the lived experiences of minoritized people in favor of a presumably "rational" set of living conditions in which the police are used to control a presumably emotional and violent BIPOC population. As I will describe in more detail in the next chapter, repairing play makes space for understanding the often violent and "emotional" affects produced by play.

The "rational" telos of the play I've described in this chapter is productive in a material and economic sense. For evidence of this, one need look no further than the burgeoning "serious games" movement. According to a survey by Sawyer and Smith (2008, 23–27), serious games have applications as diverse as health, advertisement, training, education, science, research, production, and labor. You might now find serious games in government, nongovernmental organizations, defense, health care, marketing, communication, education, business, and industry. Serious games are an extension of the prorational aspects of play and are explicitly designed to strengthen their respective fields. In other words, they are designed to reinforce the order of existing institutional frameworks.

Serious games have been particularly influential on today's game studies. This application of play is often well-meaning and altruistically minded insofar as it situates play as a potential driver for collective action. It tries to imagine a path for gaming that betters education, social justice, and even media literacy. Although serious game designers and theorists often see themselves as being allied with the struggles BIPOC people face globally, they further a vision of play that neglects the many ways that play can be traumatic. In this sense, serious play continues Huizinga's mission to compel readers to understand how play "civilizes." Civility, in his definition, aligns the interests of a mostly White, upper-class elite against the interests of BIPOC people who globally are just "making do."

Tara Fickle is wise to the ways that this cannon of play theory has neglected BIPOC interests. Huizinga, Caillois, and so many others, she argues, were Orientalists. By this, she means that they were Western scholars who, through their work, exoticized and fetishized eastern play practices. Fickle (2019) concurs with much of the aforementioned, writing that play theory defaults to a "Eurocentric viewpoint, in which 'culture' implicitly means Western European culture" (115). Thus, the work of Huizing and Caillois ultimately aims to further the White European norms, which have been seeded globally through colonial initiatives for centuries. Recognizing that play as we know it is aligned with the interests of a White bourgeois few is key to moving forward and developing a new theory of play that explores the experiences of BIPOC people.

The beginnings of such a theory are discussed today in game studies. There has been significant discourse on the topic in game studies, as there remain many game designers who continue to embrace colonialist tropes in their design practice. Critical game studies scholar Soraya Murray (2018) even suggests that there is significant interest in the field to constitute the start of a postcolonial game studies that is specifically engaged in the "lived space" of play (6). In her important work pulling together and unifying a coalition of postcolonial scholarship, Murray also identifies the gap, which this chapter hopes to have filled. Namely, postcolonial game studies scholarship is fundamentally interested in games, not play. Play considers the practices that take place in and around games, but it also includes practices that are not related to games at all. As I will describe in more detail in chapter 4, play includes things like slave songs, which were a key part of survival, hope, and tradition for Black folks on plantations. Even games like the aforementioned "Hide the Switch," which is often considered children's play, pull the brutal and visceral violence of the colonial experience out of focus. As chapter 3 will describe in detail, play that repairs aims to include painful experiences such as torture specifically because these are the experiences of play that have been imposed on colonized people for centuries. Torture was a fundamental method of coercion in the colonies, and it is through play, *not games*, that we see its lasting impact on BIPOC communities.

Souvik Mukherjee (2018), also a critical game studies scholar, hints at the radical potential of play to subvert colonialist tropes in his essay "Playing Subaltern: Video Games and Postcolonialism." He concludes his piece by explaining, "The player, whether from the erstwhile colonized countries or elsewhere, nevertheless, both writes and writes back in games that engage with the questions relating to colonialism whether he or she chooses to or not. The video game medium offers the simultaneous possibilities of subalternity, protest, elitism, and hegemony; it is the actualization by the player that results in a deeper understanding and experience of the postcolonial" (518). Here, the player's ability to occupy two critical positions, where they both "write" and "write back" in games can go by another name, play. Indeed, the logic of colonialism is determining, not determinist. I agree with Mukherjee's assessment that agency is fundamental in resisting the logic of colonialism and aspiring toward a postcolonial discourse. For me, repairing play is this aspirational approach to the postcolonial.

To repair play, or to "write back" through the ways we play, we must first endeavor to produce a space where ludic narratives can aspire to tell painful stories alongside the pleasurable. It was the pleasures of trade—exotic spices, resources, free labor—that led to colonialism as an economic paradigm. Likewise, European merchants and slavers alike were captivated by the promise of wealth through trade. In this sense, it was the affect of pleasure, its cruel promise, that led them to exploit populations and people as if they were resources in the global trade "game." Repairing play means tending to the painful aspects of this discussion. Returning to the trauma of colonialism to explode the paradigm of play from within. Yes, it is important that players enjoy agency as they engage in postcolonial play. It is imperative, though, that they use this agency to remember the abuse and trauma of colonialism. For without it, the play they engage in will haplessly collude with the colonialist impulse that reads play through the racist dynamic of "civilization" and the barbaric. Despite this, I remain optimistic that we can repair play and that doing so is key to decolonizing a space that has long exploited the labor, feelings, and experiences of BIPOC people globally.

This chapter has focused on how the White European tradition of play theory, by arguing that play is responsible for "civilization," has focused on the ways that play is pleasurable as opposed to the ways that play is painful. The painful nuance of play, in other words, threatens to undermine the argument upon which these theories are built. Play is fundamental to the social structures in whatever cultures these theorists deemed "civilized." Of course, this argument is not only fundamentally a colonialist narrative, but it's tautological as well. These two problems work together to produce a basis for play theory that is clearly White supremacist. Canonical play theory, in other words, positions play only as a positive force that plays a presumably large role in separating (presumably White European) men from animals. We the readers are supposed to fill in the appallingly White supremacist overtones. We know when play does not "civilize" by observing how cultures that are not "civilized" play. Those examples of play are then scrutinized, said to be either "not play" or, in the case of Caillois, "corrupted" play.

Thus play has been positioned as a tool of colonization, and the practices of play that are the most compatible with a colonial worldview have been lauded. These practices are the most pleasurable aspects of play: virtuous play, play that educates, and play that offers relief from work. Even the play of situationism, with its emphasis on how play can reveal the truth rather than occlude it, might be seen in this tradition. We must look to examples of play from BIPOC creators in order to repair it. As it stands, theorizing on play risks embracing colonialism by uncritically celebrating all play that is pleasurable and excluding experiences of play that are hurtful, painful, and even traumatic.

2

Play as Affect

The summer of 2016 was a joyous one for gamers. The company Niantic had just released *Pokémon GO!*, a smash hit game that let players search for Pokémon in the real world. Urban and suburban landscapes across the world were transformed as players hunted near major and minor landmarks for these elusive and rare creatures. Suddenly games, which had long been associated with couch culture and the domestic space of a gamer den or living room, had spilled out onto the streets. Some shops even offered discounts and promotions for the players who were excited about the game. It was an exciting time, as people mingled happily striking up new conversations that led to new friendships everywhere. These good vibrations, unfortunately, weren't shared by all. Game designer Omari Akil (2016) wrote a popular post for *Medium*[1] with the simple title "Warning: Pokémon GO Is Death Sentence If You Are a Black Man."

Akil was truth telling. Black men in the United States are forced to constantly assess whether or not they are welcome in White spaces. Simple things like going to a grocery store or hanging out at the mall are coded differently when you're Black. Furthermore, tragedies like 2012's murder of Trayvon Martin and 2014's murder of Michael Brown were just recent memories.[2] In the article, Akil talks about the statistical likelihood that he might be approached by the police while playing *Pokémon GO!* he talks about how he might appear threatening to police if he reaches for his identification in his back pocket and comports his body to look as "pleasant and nonthreatening as possible" (para. 7). In other words, one player's fun is another player's pain.

Pokémon GO! is an AR or "augmented reality" game. It uses the phone's camera and GPS system to track and animate Pokémon as if they were hiding in the landscape around you. Thus, to catch Pokémon, you must pull your phone out and walk around—explore your neighborhood. Akil's point is that the gameplay of *Pokémon GO!* encourages players to transgress a number of unwritten rules that Black folk adhere to for safety. Aimlessly walking around a neighborhood with your cell phone, for instance, plays into a number of stereotypes that assume that the player might be milling around looking for trouble, selling drugs, or worse. He argues that in *Pokémon GO!*, we have a game that must be played differently by people of different races.

This hard truth is both sad and difficult to process. That one game might affect different groups of people in different ways—leading to two separate experiences—is upsetting, to say the least. The importance of this conceit cannot be emphasized enough, and it applies to far more games than just *Pokémon GO!* The stakes of play are simply different. BIPOC people are subject to forms of harassment that their White counterparts are not. The weight of this othering is oppressive, and it means that we BIPOC people *play* differently. Although the experience is often still joyous, we know that it can turn on a dime. Fun can transform into fear in an instant because the unspoken rules of play assume that it is a consensual affair between White folks.

It ain't all fun and games. The affects produced by play are different for BIPOC people. We know the score. We understand the depth of play. Black folk invented the blues, after all. Moody, dark meanderings in music that are more expressive than cerebral. Play, as it stands, is not an integrated concept. If we are to repair play, we must desegregate its affective connotations—pleasure and pain. Attention to affect allows us to better locate play on the margins, in the in-between, and through felt consequences.

In the introduction, I defined affect using the terms *stimulus* and *response*, but I noted that this was a partial and incomplete definition at best. Affect studies is a wide-ranging field and is also, in part, concerned with emotion. It is a wing of phenomenology that concerns itself specifically with what one might call the structure of emotion. This implies everything from the psychology of trauma and joy, to the physiology of pleasure and pain, to the role of often invisible sensations between us that are lived and felt. This chapter takes a detour into affect studies because it affords a window into how the emotional burdens carried by BIPOC people intersect with theories of play.

To recap, I have argued that canonical theories of play have been guilty of a kind of tunnel vision that sees it as productive of pleasure but not pain. Not only is this definition troubling because of the many commonsense ways that we know play to be dangerous, harmful, and difficult, but it also excludes the narratives of BIPOC people, who have long endured pain at the expense of White European play. For example, the leisurely consumption of spices, stories, and other exotic goods in Europe encouraged colonial regimes to enslave, subjugate, and steal from BIPOC people globally. Repairing play means centering these experiences and their legacies. This means understanding the emotional burdens still carried by BIPOC people and recognizing how, for many of us, play can be as frightening as it is joyful. Affect studies affords such a window into the souls of BIPOC folk, as it offers language for discussing feeling.

There is also some scholarly merit to this work. Scholars of games have begun the work of connecting games and affect, but curiously, they stopped short of describing how *play* is productive of affects. Instead, the research they engage in examines how games produce affect in a player. Aubrey Anable's wonderful book *Playing with Feelings* opens with a montage of examples that explain well how affect can structure collective experiences. Take for example how affects of boredom and melancholy might lead to a synchronicity of play when waiting for the subway:

A woman killing time on a subway platform with *Candy Crush Saga*; commuters being alone and together while playing similar games on their phones. In such moments of being in relation through a type of signifying structure, we do not lose sight of affect; rather, this is the only possible way to make sense of it. The rest of the time it is too blurry and diffuse. At the interface, we get fragments that tell us something about the larger picture that cannot be grasped at once. A video game is such an interface for grasping a contemporary structure of feeling. (Anable 2018, xix)

Anable gives us an excellent description of how affect —which resides in the in-between—connects seemingly disparate figures behaving similarly in the same space. Commuting is boring; people react to this feeling in a variety of ways; collectively, we can see that many people escape into the games on their phones. Affect describes the entirety of this encounter. It is the boredom; it is the escape; it is the innumerable other things (napping, chatting, craving coffee) that happen within this encounter with feeling. It is also multimodal and can be used to describe the specifics of feeling—boredom for example—as well as the entirety of the experience.

Anable theorizes affect in a way that foregrounds how technology, such as video games, structure affect.

I differ from Anable's account of affect insofar as I think that the interface of the "structure of feeling" she describes isn't technology but technique. All the people sitting on the subway that Anable describes are playing with their phones. The practice of play here—focused on what Sara Ahmed would term the "happy object" of the game[3]—is what evokes pleasure. When players round a bend and encounter an inevitable paywall, it may well evoke pain. The games in the hands of the players may structure the feelings they encounter (as I return to later in this chapter when I discuss *Pokémon*), but it is play that produces the affect. To repair play, we must genuinely engage with how play is productive of affects, which can be pleasurable, painful, despairing, and melancholic.

The canon of play scholars that I critiqued in the prior chapter didn't use the term *affect* to describe play. Instead, Huizinga (1980) chose the term "disposition." He wrote that "[Play] is a stepping out of 'real' life into a temporary sphere of activity with a disposition all of its own" (8). Pretending, in other words, is what people do when they play. Importantly, for Huizinga, play is neither ordinary nor real. Thus play is a disposition toward reality; the players of a game realize that the stakes are lower and the edges are softer than they are in real life. Or at least, this is how Huizinga conceived of play. But play is not only make-believe. One person's game can be another's torment. I can remember being bullied as a child in the playground, while other kids ripped the legs off insects just for fun. Perhaps Huizinga was right when he labeled play a disposition, yet overly optimistic about the ability of people to separate fantasy from reality. Indeed, extracting play from reality undermines Huizinga's main argument that play is productive of "civilization."

Yet play is a disposition. It is an inclination to bend the rules of everyday life. What if instead of questioning the nature of "reality" Huizinga had settled for society? When we play, we inhabit worlds of feeling—visceral spaces where sensation, sensemaking, emotion, and articulation are jumbled together. It's nonsense that makes sense. The mangle of play is inscrutably affective. That play produces affective worlds—which themselves mold us as competitive, collaborative, loving, scornful, or violent—is only a starting point. From here, we might focus on the accepted sites of play to deconstruct the affordances and implications that embed play within them. Only by expanding our notions of play to include the practices of diverse populations can we navigate the blurred boundary of play spaces. It is then, and only then, that from this vantage point we can consider play as liberation, resistance, and subversion.

Sara Ahmed (2004) argues that "emotions *do things*" (119). They help us to understand the connections between people and their communities, and the subtle ways that these invisible lines of affect drive bodies to action. Part of what emotions do, according to affect theory scholar Teresa Brennan (2004), is to provide refuge from the rational. The Cartesian dualism (or "mind-body split") means that we flee one for the other in times of stress. In other words, Brennan argues that when one must overcome an overwhelming feeling in their body, they flee to the cold calculus of the mind for relief (Brennan 2004, 23). The aforementioned scholars of play have also struggled to reconcile this dualism. Play is theorized through embodiment, and games are associated with rationality. Children flinging their bodies around the playground are associated with play, whereas games are more cerebral—chess strategy comes to mind. The split, of course, is hogwash. Emotion is just as much a part of our mind as it is our body. What's more, this split has long been used to reinforce White supremacy by associating BIPOC people with the body and White folk with the mind. Research on affect aims to valorize the experiences of women and people of color by shining a light upon how central emotion, sensation, and embodiment are to our day-to-day lives.

By considering affect, the concept of play better speaks to the experiences of BIPOC people. Consider the customs and rules that we bend when we mourn a loved one: a day off from work, an excuse not to smile, isolation for days, allowances within one's community for the overindulgence of spirits. This, of course, is the dark side of play. Repairing play is that which deals with regret, sadness, and anger. It is the moment when the social contract is breached through entropy instead of enthusiasm and joy. We have the colloquialism "playing hooky" to describe skipping work to partake in leisure, yet we simply describe the opposite as "mourning." In both, we play with cultural norms. In both, we pursue different affects.

Sadness is key to understanding the affective state of BIPOC people. We are haunted by the ghosts of our ancestors. I admire how Ann Cvetkovich encourages us to engage with how the memorialization of trauma is productive of affect. She terms this an "emotional color line," and uses playwright Anna Deveare Smith's depiction of philosopher Cornel West to define it. Smith wrote *Twilight: Los Angeles, 1992*, in the wake of the LA riots that followed the Rodney King verdict. Cvetkovich (2012) summarizes the "emotional color line" in terms of meritocracy, survival, and trauma. She writes, "[West] suggests that sadness comes when the belief that one should be happy or protected turns out to be wrong and when a privileged form of hopefulness that has so often been entirely foreclosed for black people is punctured" (116). Black sadness, in other words, is a condition endemic to Black people drawn from centuries of bondage, torture, and suffering. Repairing play must engage with Black sadness if it is to be reparative. Thus it is essential to mark and recognize the ways that play might produce pain.

José Muñoz (2006) describes brown affect in a similar way. He describes brown feeling as an "ethic of the self" and uses it to discuss what it means for BIPOC people to survive in White society. I sit writing now in a majority

White coffee shop in a gentrified neighborhood. Music from White bands plays on a speaker, and I listen to gleeful chatter from the folks around me. All the while, I feel out of place. I wonder how these strangers might react if I struck up a conversation. I wonder if my father could have inhabited a similar space fifty years ago? All in all, it bums me out. Yet, I spy another BIPOC individual working alone and am comforted knowing that I am not alone in this sadness. The alienation I just described, as well as the solidarity in sadness, are "brown feeling" (676). As established in the prior chapter, the typical affect produced by play is that of pleasure, it is an affect closely tied to White "civilization." The "brown feeling" that Muñoz describes is an ethic that is intended to locate a common ground among BIPOC people. The sense of belonging found within the depression that he and West describe is reparative because it recognizes how the violence of racism is systemic. Repair means more than identifying villains; it means recognizing how the ideology of what bell hooks (2010) terms "imperialist White-supremacist capitalist patriarchy" (para. 2) divides and turns everyone against one another.

An understanding of play that comprehends the concept as productive of affect can better help us grasp how play relates to systems of oppression. Even when play is productive of pleasure, it may be masking layered social trauma beneath. Take postindustrial Japan's embrace of precarious labor, or the gig and service economy, as an example. Japan's embrace of precarity[4] has led to a generation of hopeless-feeling, despairing youth. Kids working low-paying service jobs feel terrible inhabiting their day-to-day routines and escape to the vibrant and pleasurable worlds of games to escape. Thus the social demand for affect is now at a premium, and the advertising and entertainment industries have exploited this market.

Critical media scholar Anne Allison (2009) describes the affective appeal of *Pokémon*. For her, *Pokémon* is both an instance of soft, affective power—the power of attraction, the promise of escape—and a global economic product (96–7). It succeeds, in part, because of the labor of its participants. The ability for friends to communicate with one another, trade, and compare Pokémon encourages the proliferation of Pokémon as a platform. In other words, Pokémon sells because it rewards its consumers. It provides a fantasy experience that is integrated into the very fabric of everyday life. The fantasy is a positive one—designed to help pull players into an affectively pleasurable context of play.

The affective context of play—pleasure and pain—is also crucial to understanding the inclusivity of play spaces, as well as who is hailed when play is invoked. As Ahmed (2004) points out in her work on the economies of affect, "My argument is not that there is a psychic economy of fear that then becomes social and collective: rather, the individual subject comes into being through its very alignment with the collective. *It is the very failure of affect to be located in a subject or object that allows it to generate the surfaces of collective bodies"* (128, italics mine). Feeling down. Feeling brown. Some kind of blue. These fragmented feelings are distributed and shared communally. How players identify with the collective mood, or (to borrow from Muñoz) disidentify with it, informs the collective subjectivity of BIPOC players today (1999, 5–6).

Returning to Anna Deveare Smith's vocalization of West, the disidentification with the pleasures of meritocracy that constitute the conditions of Whiteness is a part of the story of Black people in North America. The White American dream of a stable income, middle-class home, and safe neighborhood denies identification with a common history of discrimination, struggle, and bondage. The erasure of torture and other painful tonalities of play from game design is intimately tied to the theorization of play advanced by a canon of White European scholars. Inclusivity means more than tending to representation; it also means tending to the stories that the games we play tell, and the texture of the experiences that they provide. Play that is inclusive of BIPOC people must work to conjure moods of joy, exuberance, and excitement alongside the traumatic, painful, and torturous.

For those looking to design inclusive games, the insights shared in this chapter are undoubtedly tricky to navigate. On the one hand, recognizing how painful experiences can bring depth to game design opens up portions of one's creative palette that were previously inaccessible. On the other hand, designing interactive experiences that are painful and traumatic runs counter to many of the genre tropes many have come to accept when consuming games. This impasse is real, and I can admit that I don't know an easy way to navigate it. The uneasiness many of us have in confronting a broad spectrum of feelings is part of the point.

Repairing play is that which, like the BIPOC people it centers, cannot be at home in any one affect or feeling. It is imperative to recognize the ways that the affective and the aesthetic work together to produce evocative experiences. Muñoz's work on brown feeling recognizes how recognizing, discussing, and understanding feelings such as depression can be a common point of solidarity and community. The point is not just that feeling out of place is difficult; it is also that from this difficulty new potential forms of community can emerge. By focusing on the uneasy and difficult affects that play can produce, we open the door to new and radical forms of community. These new and emergent forms of community foreground the shared histories of imperialism, oppression, slavery, and torture that unite BIPOC people across the globe. We know the importance of sorrow, lamentation, and pain. These low affects must be foregrounded alongside joy, fun, and pleasure as we strive to repair play. By imagining a kind of play that

runs the affective gamut, we imagine a potential play
that is less captivating, more sincere, and ultimately
more inclusive. In other words, repairing play courts
resistance by promising more than mere fun—it flirts
with difficult and undesirable feelings—thus it is decid-
edly against the capture of our attention, bodies, and
money within its aesthetic.

3
Play as Capture

This is America
Don't catch you slippin' now
Look at how I'm livin' now
Police be trippin' now
Yeah, this is America
Guns in my area
I got the strap
I gotta carry 'em
                    —Childish Gambino, "This Is America"

Ten children walk in a playground casually chatting. One of them reaches out to another and cries, "You're it!" The tagged child lunges in a desperate bid to rid themselves of the stigma by touching another. Soon the group scatters and a melee ensues. The game is tag, and its very grammar suggests that even innocent play may well be a violent activity. The game divides players into subjects and objects. Once a player is tagged, they are driven to reconcile their situation by tagging someone else. The game's vernacular reduces players to a status of an "other" or even object; like it or not, they are "it." The word "it" implies less than human. "It" has been fundamental to the lexicon of bigotry and White supremacy in America since before the American Revolutionary War. The very basis of "it" equivocates humanness with objectness, as it strips "it" from the fundamental rights granted to other subjects. One does not consent to play tag, nor does one offer their consent to become "it" in tag. This, the simplest of games, reveals play is not a relationship between subjects. Instead, it is a relationship between subject and object.

Like Childish Gambino says, "This is America." A place where being Black has long been equated with being less than human. The wealthy and White here get access to leisure, while the poor and Black are left to toil in the fields. A place where George Floyd's final words, "I can't breathe," were heard as if he was an object. A place where the cops allow Kyle Rittenhouse, a seventeen-year-old White kid, to walk away after unloading an M15 rifle into a group of Black Lives Matter protesters. There are different rules for different people here. In America's playground, Black folks are always "it." When you break it down, play means different things for different people. Unfortunately, play for White folk can often be torturous and even deadly to Black folk.

The relationship between torture and play relies on the question of consent. Play, as many contemporary game design theorists have argued, is a fundamentally consensual relationship (Salen and Zimmerman 2004, 474; Stenros and Bowman 2018, 417). Because consent is central to most scholarly definitions of play, we are left with the paradox explained in the introduction where consensual torture satisfies a definition of play while nonconsensual torture does not. The examples they offer to justify this distinction are almost always formal. They speak more to a desire of what play *should be* rather than from an observation of what play *is*. Do we negotiate consent when we play with a computer or with ourselves? Play mediates in ways that are not as straightforward or confined as they may seem at first. In fact, interrogating the mediatory force of play challenges us to reconcile the violence that lies at the heart of innumerable social relationships.

The consensual relationship structured by play often works through another term: *negotiation*. As Miguel Sicart (2014) explains, "We play by negotiating the purposes of play, how far we want to extend the influences of the play activity, and how much we play for the purpose of playing or for the purpose of personal expression" (16). Here, Sicart nests the idea of negotiation within the concept of play, building on the prior work of Jesper Juul, who sought to locate the idea of negotiation within the concept of the game. For Juul, all games have negotiable consequences (2005, 36). Negotiation thus differentiates between what is a game and what is war. Distinguishing whether negotiation is considered fundamental to play or games reflects a broader

understanding of the consensuality of each phenomenon. To negotiate assumes that each player respects the
other's ideas, positions, and sovereignty. When players negotiate, they treat one another as fellow humans,
and not as objects. Yet, so often play defies negotiation.
David Leonard argues that in sports video games, in
which the presumed White player is invited to take on
the role of Black athletes without being forced to live
through the trauma of Black experience, play is not
negotiated (Leonard 2004, para. 5). The Black community has not consented to this form of identity tourism,
yet this sort of minstrelsy is a common form of play.
Negotiation is more of an ideal than an observed reality
in games and play today.

Repairing play starts from the premise that play is
not necessarily reciprocal. If play is not reciprocal, then
it becomes obvious how play itself is power. Back to the
playground. The bullies tease, mock, and even fight
with other children. They are all playing, but it per-
sists because of the bully's whims. When I use the term
repairing play, I am arguing for an approach to play that
recognizes how painful the status quo of play is for so
many BIPOC people. For without understanding the
trauma lurking in the center of play, one cannot antici-
pate and work to assuage it.

Other scholars concur that not all play is consensual.
Here I want to signal my appreciation of scholarship
that acknowledges how the assumed norms of consent
that are hailed by the "magic circle of play" are often

transgressed by White men. In her autoethnographic writing, Emma Vossen explains, "Unfortunately, because of contemporary practices surrounding gameplay, most video gameplay that I have participated in has contained practices that were not consensual or enjoyable, such as harassment, gender-based insults, or trash talk" (Vossen 2018, 206). Appreciating how play is wielded as an instrument of power begins by recognizing accounts of play that would otherwise be lost in a definition that presumes voluntary participation.

My argument relies on three premises. First, drawing on the work of Johan Huizinga (1980), I argue that play is voluntary if you are the player (7). Second, building on the historical work of Clifford Geertz and recent scholarship by Miguel Sicart, I concur that play is a "way of being" (Geertz 1972; Sicart 2014). Third, I build on the proposition laid forth by Roger Caillois's (2001) work that play is not necessarily voluntary for the played (52). Based on these premises, if play is voluntary for the player, but not necessarily voluntary for the played, then play is a subject–object relationship and not a subject–subject relationship. Following a subject–object orientation, then torture is a form of play, even in its most brutal and disgusting forms.

Importantly, this chapter crystallizes the aforementioned logical conjuncture through the metaphor of policing. Given the larger premise that play is often torture for those who are its object, I think it is crucial to draw parallels between it and law enforcement. In every game, there is a player who remembers and enforces the rules, a rule cop,[1] so to speak. The lens of policing helps to drive home the point that play is often one-sided. Will a bully relent if his victim gasps, "I can't breathe?" We know that the rules of the playground are different for kids with different backgrounds. Indeed, the language of law enforcement helps to underscore the point: play is often brutal, one-sided, unfair, and punishing.

Play Arrests

In this section, I juxtapose the concept of arrest—the ability to cease the free movement of another body—against the concept of voluntarism. Arrest helps to reveal, through the language of discipline and policing, that the voluntarism of play is a one-sided affair. Huizinga's original theorization of the term argued strongly that voluntarism was a key aspect of play. I believe that this is true for only one of the many parties engaging in play. Like a police arrest, which is voluntary for the police, I argue that the power relationship construed by play is similar. Play captivates; it captures. And when we play, we capitulate.

The idea that play is voluntary has been a fundamental part of play theory since Johan Huizinga penned *Homo Ludens*. Huizinga (1980) writes,

> First and foremost, then, all play is a voluntary
> activity. Play to order is no longer play: it could be

at best a forcible imitation of it. By this quality of freedom alone, play marks itself off from the course of the natural process. It is something added thereto and spread out over it like a flowering, an ornament, a garment. Obviously, freedom must be understood here in the wider sense that leaves untouched the philosophical problem of determinism. It may be objected that this freedom does not exist for the animal and the child; they *must* play because their instinct drives them to it and because it serves to develop their bodily faculties and their powers of selection. . . . Child and animal play because they enjoy playing, and therein precisely lies their freedom. (Huizinga 1980, 7–8)

When Huizinga argues that play is essentially a voluntary activity, he compares animal and child play. He specifically considers these categories because, as he articulates, children are yet to develop the rational faculties we attribute to adult humans. He is wary that the subjectivities of children and animals may be different than that of adults, and thus they may be driven to play by instinct. It's worth noting here that comparisons to animals have long been a White supremacist tactic used to dehumanize BIPOC. I make this comparison because—as I will argue in more depth later—the experience of Blackness holds remarkable similarities with the experience of play. We can find these similarities in Huizinga's comparison of children and animals.

Despite these comparisons, it's important to note here that voluntarism implies that every participant in a game is a player. But what if someone decides they don't want to play, such as in the example of tag posed earlier? In this example, if one acts as a spoilsport and chooses not to play after they are tagged, they still become "it." In other words, Huizinga uses terms like *spoilsport* to allow for play practices where one voluntarily opts out of the play space. What he doesn't account for are play practices that pull the spoilsport back to the game table even after they have flipped it. After all, a price is paid when one refuses to play.

The spoilsport is a figure who has been violently arrested by play and refuses its discipline. Sara Ahmed's killjoy is a paradigm example of this case. The killjoy "flips the table" after being subjected to the patriarchal diatribes of her family. She kills the joy of her father, the patriarch, because she aims to resist the discipline of patriarchy. Yet, she is disciplined by him (and the rest of the family) for this act of resistance. She is arrested by play, despite her desire to leave the game altogether.

The suggestion that play is voluntary neglects all the instances in which it is not. It presents a radically subjective vision of play instead of one that is always-already constrained by a shifting set of social relationships and experiences. The spoilsport still engages in play even if they don't engage with the game.[2] By recognizing that play is only voluntary for the individual initiating play, we demystify the spoilsport by showing how their violence toward the game may be a result of another player's violence toward them and their feelings. This contradiction, that play is voluntary for some yet not for others, confounds Huizinga's theory of play. His is a romantic vision that idealizes the voluntary.

Play is not voluntary for those who are objectified through it. Yet, in all cases here—that of the child, other, and animal—pleasure is offered as the primary explanation for what drives individuals to play. In pleasure, we find a common link between the actions of subjects and the actions of objects. If we are to understand how objects play, we must consider, as Miguel Sicart does, the relationship between play and pleasure.

Captivity and Play

Moving away from an instrumental understanding of play, which defines play as an activity, Miguel Sicart (2014) posits that play is a way of being that exists within all activity (6). Sicart's work is a sharp turn away from Huizinga's approach to play. Extended by Katie Salen and Eric Zimmerman (2004, 95), a neo-Huizingan approach suggests that play thrives in ritual spaces marked as distinct from everyday life. Although the opacity of the magic circle has been questioned by many, a neo-Huizingan approach still provides a compelling foil for Sicart's philosophy. He suggests that play exists within all things, but is often focused during events, within play-objects (like games), and in particular spaces. But what if this phenomenology of play as being is itself a form of captivity? When we play, are we not back on the slave ship, captured and waiting in the hold?

Play as being extends and generalizes Huizinga's theory that play is productive of "civilization." It suggests that play is a necessary part of what it means to know oneself as a person. If play is being, then it is a condition that everyone is caught up in. Thus it is also captivity. BIPOC folks know this. Here in the cage of society, there is a hierarchy that enforces the rules. It's the values of White society that the police are made to enforce.

Play as captivity prompts a rethinking of questions that have long generated curiosity in the field of game studies. There has long been a scholarly thread fascinated with the seemingly paradoxical similarities between labor and leisure. Are professional athletes working or playing? Is the slog of video game playtesting leisure at all? These questions all play on a binary distinction between labor and leisure. Recognizing that play has encircled and arrested both concepts has great explanatory power here. Understanding play as captivity speaks better to the painful aspects of play in everyday life.

In his definition of play, Sicart suggests several characteristics that this mode of being takes on. Play is contextual, he argues, and varies in degree by circumstance. It is carnivalesque—a way of challenging traditional understandings of status and power. Sicart also argues that play is appropriative, suggesting that it can latch on to almost any circumstance and transform it. Finally, and most salient to this book's arguments about torture, Sicart argues that play is pleasurable:

> It is pleasurable but the pleasures it creates are not always submissive to enjoyment, happiness, or positive traits. Play can be pleasurable when it hurts, offends, challenges us and teases us, and even when we are not playing. Let's not talk about play as fun but as pleasurable, opening us to the immense variations of pleasure in this world. (Sicart 2014, 3)

The comparison of pleasure and fun helps us understand how play exists in the world. If we look at play as pleasure as opposed to fun, we turn away from the rhetoric of play as progress that defines it as a positive activity. Some forms of play, such as BDSM, are often considered pleasurable as opposed to fun. What's more, BDSM highlights how torture is commonly accepted as a pleasurable form of play. Following this line of reasoning, should brutal, disciplinary torture also be considered play? Traditional scholars of play would draw the line here. Yet, I feel these approaches to play are naive. Although there is a strong sentiment that the phenomenology of play is wholly positive, we know from the feminist accounts, such as Vossen's noted earlier, that this is far from the truth. Thus, I argue that brutal, disciplinary torture is always (unfortunately) a form of play, and this definition is wholly consistent with Sicart's understanding of the term. To argue this, I draw a distinction between the player and the played.

This distinction is significant because it encourages us to rethink how we classify others in multiplayer games.

Policing Play

The distinction between the player and the played has been invisibly policed in play scholarship. It is best brought to focus by Roger Caillois in the introduction to *Man, Play, and Games*, as he considers the historical circumstance of Huizinga's work. Caillois attributes the curious omission of games in Huizinga's work on play to the somewhat sordid connotations they had in early twentieth-century society. Because Huizinga sought to construct a theory of play that would show how all "civilized" society related to the concept, he was forced to omit games with connotations of street life and gambling. Caillois (2001) argues that if Huizinga was to include morally dubious games in his theory of play, he would undermine his assertion that all civilization springs from play (5). Hence, the moral gray area of gambling undermines the premise of civility that Huizinga's play is premised upon. In other words, games are accepted as an invisible and thus inconsequential part of the play phenomenon.

Caillois's work continues this mode of policing. If gambling is a morally dubious activity for some, then the bloody and sordid affair of warfare is as well. As I described in more detail in chapter 2, Caillois's worked hard to disambiguate forms of play that he felt were constructive from those he felt were corrupted. Just as the police discipline citizens as they divide and judge whether their behavior is criminal, Caillois's work polices the concept of play itself. In making a case for how war functions as a game, Caillois adds a caveat to war's most brutal and amoral characteristics. War is a game, Caillois (2001) argues, but when brutal, it is play that has been corrupted:

> Various restrictions on violence fall into disuse. Operations are no longer limited to frontier provinces, strongholds, and military objectives. They are no longer conducted according to a strategy that once made war itself resemble a game. War is far removed from the tournament or duel, i.e. from regulated combat in an enclosure, and now finds its fulfillment in massive destruction and the massacre of entire populations. (Caillois 2001, 55)

Play arrests some players, while others get to hand out tickets. Play is not necessarily voluntary for those it objectifies. Caillois's awareness of this is visible in his remarks that brutal moments of war are a "corrupted" form of competition. While Huizinga reserved that moments of grotesque and extreme warfare ceased to be play (Huizinga 1980, 9), Caillois recovers a conversation about play and games free of what he considered arbitrary delineations about what could not be play in Huizinga's work, such as between gambling and non-gambling. The victims of war do not volunteer. Nor does the object of abuse in "Hide the Switch." In both examples, play has turned grizzly and corrupt. Although there have been attempts to make the violence of play invisible, I argue that it is important to recognize how the rhetoric of play polices what is and is not considered a game. When we neglect what Caillois refers to as the corrupt aspects of play, we participate in policing that removes BIPOC from the discourse around play and games.

Play Is a Subject–Object Relationship

In this chapter, I have deliberately invoked the language of policing and to some extent, discipline in an effort to subvert a commonsense understanding of play as voluntary. Play is voluntary, but only to the players who initiate the experience. Play polices, it arrests, and it captures others on a whim. By theorizing play as a relationship to captivity, we might begin to make space for people who previously have been victims of one of play's cruel games.

This chapter has been an attempt to justify three premises that lead to the conclusion that play is a subject–object relationship. I argue that play is voluntary for the player but not the played. Play is a way of being in the world rather than an activity. Together, these stances lead us to the understanding that play is not necessarily voluntary for the played. One concern that one might have at this point is that the played does not necessarily occupy an object position; therefore, play is not necessarily a subject–object relationship. For example, if both participants in tag willingly engage one another in the game, play is then a subject–subject relationship and therefore a consensual relationship.

This counterexample is important because it highlights a simple way that my argument can be misunderstood. I am not arguing that either player in this example loses a sense of subjectivity (or an ability to consent) when played with. I am instead arguing that neither characteristic necessarily defines play. Toward my desire to repair play, it is necessary to locate play as not necessarily a relationship that inherently invokes consent. When we play, we transform others and the world around us into play-objects. The destructive and violent aspects of play emerge from this transformation and must be contended with if we are to understand the term.

The definition of play as a subject–object relationship leaves us with a new paradox to contend with. If play is a subject–object relationship, how should one reconcile their own subjective experience with the fact that through play they will be treated as an object? To answer this question of what it means to objectify one's self, we must turn to philosophy concerned with the phenomenon of double consciousness and the Black experience.

Perhaps the metaphor of policing will be enough to make the theory in this chapter intriguing to designers.

So much of play theory today imagines play as a form of freedom, and this chapter encourages us to imagine it as the opposite. Did you think play was fun? It can be torture! Did you think play was freedom? It's captivity, arrest. I reiterate these points because they allow designers the creative freedom to design against the muscular power fantasies that characterize so many games today. As the cultural crises we contend with here in America remind us, a White person's freedom is a Black person's death sentence. This is America, after all.

4
Torture and the Black American Experience

But I keeps laughin'
Instead of cryin'
I must keep fightin'
Until I'm dyin'
And Ol' Man River
He just keeps rolling along!
　　　　　—Paul Robeson, "Ol' Man River," 1938

I grew up a mixed-race kid in a suburban New Jersey home. My White and Jewish mom was from Long Island, while my Black and spiritual dad grew up on a farm in a small town called Cream Ridge. My dad's father, Grandpa Web, was in the army, stationed in Nuremberg during the trials, right before my dad was born. In the army, he was a cook (and later a drill sergeant), so when he returned home, he would feed all six of his kids like they were soldiers in a mess hall. When my father's parents moved to New Jersey, they built their shed out of military surplus: army crates and bricks scrounged from the base. My grandfather, like many men of his generation, was particularly hard on his children. My father and his siblings eventually came to terms with my grandfather and forgave him, despite his rough edges. I disagree with their unqualified forgiveness but understand why they are sympathetic. I sometimes cook up his BBQ sauce in the summer to remember him.

My father has worn many hats over the course of his life. He's been a conscientious objector who fled the National Guard, college dropout, weed dealer, short-order cook, inventor, union man, and even politician. He was the first Black man to be elected to the executive board of I.A.T.S.E. Local 52. In this union organization, he ran the video department alongside the Italian and Irish families who had helped run it since the early golden age of film. They called him names, sabotaged his equipment, and made him haul heavy equipment up the narrow stairwells of Manhattan. My dad was the back door to the I.A.T.S.E. film union for about two decades, helping BIPOC people find good-paying work in an industry that still operated somewhere between a family business and the mob. New York's jazz station, WBGO, was always on in his office. I remember it filling the air with the sound of John Coltrane, Max Roach, Miles Davis, Ella Fitzgerald, and Duke Ellington. Yet I also still remember how my dad bristled after I taunted him in my adolescence and asserted, "I'm not your slave!"

The term "slave" had been normalized for me through casual conversations with my friends. It was also embedded in the fantasy literature I was consuming and the science fiction movies I was watching. The White, middle-class world I inhabited generally didn't see the word as a problem. For my father, it was triggering. When he heard it, his tone shifted and his brows furrowed. I can still visualize the gentle pain in his eyes as he admonished me for using it so glibly. My mom, sister, and I were all upset by the mood that would be brought into the room. My mom would later describe it with one simple and deeply stereotypical word: "anger." I know now that it was trauma: the trauma of colonization, of slavery, all caught up in Blackness. My dad was working through that which had disciplined him as a child. He was caught up in the pain of throwing himself against the bars of a White suburban world that had long forgotten the trauma of slavery, while also demanding that he forget it too. I learned what it meant to be Black in that conversation. I learned how to carry my father's burden even as I traversed White society. My own family history reflects how BIPOC people manage the violence of colonialism. We, like many others, were forced to manage the trauma of being placed on the slave ship.

Others have written about the slave ship experience better than I ever could. Famously, W.E.B. Du Bois (1994) wrote *The Souls of Black Folk* in an attempt to explain the unique experience of Black Americans. He

conceptualizes the Black experience through the metaphor of the veil, where an individual must reconcile
their identity through two lenses: (1) a projection of
how they appear within society (how the veil appears
to others) and (2) a historic and communal understanding of the self (life behind the veil). He refers to
this as "double consciousness," or a "sense of always
looking at one's self through the eyes of others, of mea-
suring one's soul by the tape of a world that looks on
in amused contempt and pity" (Du Bois 1994, 5). The
depth of experience to which Du Bois refers is a result
of the dehumanization wrought by slavery. Even in
America today, Black folk are constantly negotiating stereotypes that conspire to reduce them to objects. They
remain forced to occupy and negotiate positions of both
subject and object through their experiences of double
consciousness.

The prior chapter established that repairing play
acknowledges how torture, however taboo, is a form of
play like all others. By centering torture and the histories of BIPOC folk like myself who cannot escape the
narratives of torture that still haunt us, we can come to
appreciate torture, pain, slavery, and discipline as a history that provides a new foundation for understanding
play. Play constantly reminds us of how simple it is
to belittle and dehumanize people. It is a constant
reminder of how subjectivity, and thus personhood, is
fragile and socially negotiated. Cruel words become terrible jokes with a simple twist of the tongue. Play teases,

torments, and toys with people as if they were simple objects. And, in a dark irony, play is celebrated for doing just this. These vertiginous edges are the basis of satire, comedy, and even theater.

Repairing play means understanding how the experience of torture relates to the Black American experience. I do this by considering torture on both societal and individual levels. By exploring torture within and across these two levels, this book prompts a discussion of play that recenters Black people within conversations about play and games and charts a course toward a radical reconstitution of torture within all of our understandings of play and games.

State-Sponsored Torture

Torture, as part of the institution of slavery, is a disciplinary mechanism of dehumanization. Just as Huizinga and Caillois categorized certain forms of destructive and barbaric play as corrupt (or not "civilized"), the philosophy of torture contends with these same boundaries. William Schultz (2007) notes them when defining torture in his collection *The Phenomenon of Torture: Readings and Commentary*:

> Somehow inflicting pain on a creature is less acceptable, less "civilized" than doing away with them altogether. That is why we go to great lengths to make sure that the process of capital execution is as sterile

and painless as possible. If we actually appeared to be enjoying another's suffering, if we indulged too openly that part of us that revels in revenge on those who do us wrong, we would see something about ourselves mighty important to keep hidden. The State is meant to be a projection of our values, a mirror of our best selves, and hence, though the State may do away with criminals, it may not gloat in their demise. (Schultz 2007, 8)

Schultz's critique relates mainly to state-sponsored torture, such as that performed by US military personnel on Iraqis in the detention camp at Abu Ghraib. Although torture transgresses boundaries, in warfare, torture is policed. Just as Huizinga and Caillois sought to exclude games that would turn violent or exploit vulnerable populations, Schultz and Méndez illustrate how torture is policed during warfare. All pretenses of civility in matters of both play and war must be abandoned when torture is invoked. Despite this unfortunate conclusion, the practice of torture lies at the heart of both.

Michael Foucault's (1977) *Discipline and Punish* begins with a discussion of torture. The book, often remembered for its discussion of panopticism, opens with a vignette of a man being drawn and quartered in mid-eighteenth-century France. He describes the act in detail to invoke a contrast between the seen and the unseen: "Then the executioner, his sleeves rolled up, took the steel pincers, which had been especially made for the occasion, and which were about a foot and a half long, and pulled first at the calf of the right leg, then at the thigh, and from there at the two fleshy parts of the right arm; then at the breasts" (Foucault 1977, 3–4). Torture, which used to be an act of public spectacle, still exerted a social and behavioral pressure upon social bodies by the time of his writing in the late twentieth century. It had merely been rendered invisible in most Western societies.

The crucial lesson of *Discipline and Punish* is that although torture has been made invisible, the threat of torture lingers within social institutions as a mode of social control. The spotlight of Bentham's watchtower shines upon prisoners to occlude the shape of the guards monitoring their behavior (Foucault 1977, 201). By extension, the threat of torture is omnipresent. We must consider whether games also act as a similar disciplinary apparatus, concealing the possibility of torture within mere play. Is it possible that when we begin a game that a hint of danger lies beneath the supposed connotations of fun? After all, if the object of the challenge were to decline to participate, they might be labeled stubborn or a "bad sport."

Intimate Torture

Of course, Foucault's writing on torture is not limited only to theories of the state. In *The History of Sexuality*, he notes that torture is used in tandem with confession as a way of understanding another body's sexuality.

Torture and confession became mechanisms for extracting truth from people: "Since the Middle Ages, torture has accompanied [confession] like a shadow, and supported [confession] when it could go no further: the dark twins" (Foucault 1978, 59). For Foucault, in this sense, objective truth does not exist. Truth becomes a vector of power and confession a technique of disciplining the self. Du Bois also contends with torture in this personal, intimate sense. He explains how torture was used as a method for extracting the truth from slaves. Intimate torture relates specifically to how truth is gathered from people seen as less-than-human objects.

The slave's body is an extension of the master's body, explains Page Du Bois,[1] relating the phenomenon of torture to the Black American experience. In her book *Torture and Truth*, she draws on an Aristotelian construction to show how the apparatus of torture reduced Black slaves to an object:

> The slave is a part of the master—he is, as it were, a part of the body, alive but yet separated from it. ([Aristotle], *Politics* 1255b)

> Thus, according to Aristotle's logic, representative or not, the slave's truth is the master's truth; it is in the body of the slave that the master's truth lies, and it is in torture that his truth is revealed. The torturer reaches through the master to the slave's body, and extracts the truth from it. (Du Bois 2007, 14)

Through Aristotle's writing, Page Du Bois shrewdly points both to the association of the slave (and therefore Black people generally) with the body—made an object through a traditional understanding of the Cartesian dualism—and its intimate relationship with the master. The slave becomes the object (body) in a relationship where the master is the subject (mind). This understanding of torture and truth is mirrored in the player-played relationship where the player takes on the role of subject, and the played adopts the role of object.

As to what truth is extracted through the intimate relations of torture-play, BDSM becomes an interesting practice to consider. Is truth derived from torture indicative of one's sexuality? BDSM play, as theorized by many within the game studies community,[2] is far removed from the experience of Black people descended from slaves. It is very different than the torture that Page Du Bois describes. Torture, according to Du Bois, is always a violent expression. Practices around safe words within the BDSM community allow players the space to practice torture—albeit a softer and more socially appropriate form of torture than that which is practiced by the military—without accidentally harming one another. This book reads interventions such as safe words as an intervention intended to blunt the dangerous, toxic, and harmful potentials of play. Importantly, in the spaces of toxic gameplay highlighted by theorists like Vossen (2018) and Gray (2012), no safe word exists to extract minoritized people from abusive conversations with White men. Sadly, I feel that this lack only furthers the previous points that play is not a voluntary activity. By getting in touch with its traumatic aspects and shared histories of pain, we engage in the difficult work of repairing play.

Some might quibble with the earlier comparison, arguing that BDSM is not actual torture but instead "torture." Because in its ideal form, BDSM is consensual; it is categorically different than practices like waterboarding. In this sense, a skeptic might argue that BDSM is a form of play while reserving "torture" for disciplinary military activity. Discussions such as this miss the point. Again, they argue that the difference between play and torture alike is volunteerism. As I have argued in chapter 3, volunteerism is a form of social privilege that is not necessary to play's definition. Torture is play because play is not always voluntary. Even innocent forms of torture, such as tickle torture, don't assume a consensual relationship between the parties involved.

Slave Songs

Slave songs—also known as spirituals, sorrow songs, and jubilees—were improvisational songs that Black slaves sang with one another. They are read and understood today as simultaneously resistance and spirituality. They are resistance insofar as their meanings were illegible to the slavers who held them captive and spiritual because they evoked strong emotions between the Black folk who sang and listened to them. They were the Church, so to speak, of Black kinship on the plantation. For the purposes of my argument in this book, it is vital that we understand the importance of slave songs against the backdrop of torture. The spirituality of slave songs was, in fact, produced by the hopeless conditions within which slaves were kept. They are sullen, painful, and lamenting. They are play both because they memorialize the most painful aspects of torture and because they are improvisational performance.

Many historians and critical race theorists look to Fredrick Douglass's book *Narrative of the Life of Frederick Douglass, An American Slave* for a firsthand account of the conditions of slavery. Douglass, who escaped slavery and sought refuge in the northern United States, describes the slave songs sung on plantations:

> [Slave songs] told a tale of woe which was then altogether beyond my feeble comprehension; they were tones loud, long, and deep; they breathed the prayer and complaint of souls boiling over with the bitterest anguish. Every tone was a testimony against slavery, and a prayer to God for deliverance from chains. The hearing of those wild notes always depressed my spirit, and filled me with ineffable sadness. I have frequently found myself in tears while hearing them. The mere recurrence to those songs, even now, afflicts me; and while I am writing these lines, an expression of feeling has already found its

way down my cheek. To those songs I trace my first
glimmering conception of the dehumanizing character
of slavery. I can never get rid of that conception. Those
songs still follow me, to deepen my hatred of slavery,
and quicken my sympathies for my brethren in bonds
(Douglass 1845, 11–12).

Douglass goes on to describe how "slaves sing most
when they are most unhappy," and that the songs bring
relief, "only as an aching heart is relieved by its tears"
(Douglass, 12) Douglass's account of slave songs has an
affective and visceral impact upon the listener. The context of Douglass's account cannot be forgotten. As Jennifer Stoever (2016) notes, he prepared his book as an
effort to educate White readers about the contexts and
trauma of slavery. As such, Douglass's goal in making
slave songs legible was part of an effort to "challenge his
white readership to listen beyond their racialized expectations and desires" (49). This outreach is a plea for common ground: an effort to mobilize the play of sound in
order to broker empathy with the White public.

Importantly, the slave songs evoke tears in Douglass
because they encourage him to remember the conditions of torture within which he was raised. The play
of torture and the play of slave songs overlap. Both
evoke tears for the same affective and visceral reasons.
Yet, unlike torture, the slave song is reparative because
it offers relief. It repackages the torturous and opens an
avenue for singers and listeners to process their pain.
Like a vaccine, this therapy pulls on a small amount of

the painful, brutal, and torturous to aid the listener in working through their past pain.

Instruments and Play

In the English language, one can "play" an instrument, but they do not "play" when they sing. Perhaps this is because play is implied. As I have argued in chapter 3, play is a relationship between subject and object. So it is grammatically correct to apply the term to the objects that are played with, like the guitar, saxophone, and drums. When singing, the instrument is the body, so the English language implies play in the term "sing." What is interesting in this grammatical construction is how the English language encourages a sensibility around play that stops short of recognizing how the term turns subjects into objects. Perhaps the only two linguistic constructions of play in English that read the body as object are the phrases "playing with myself" and "playing on my heartstrings"—slang for masturbation and sympathy, respectively. Common to both is the idea that play should be affectively vivid—a motif this book has already highlighted. Reinforcing my larger point, play is either pleasure or pain.

I return to the terms *linguistic connotations* because I feel that they highlight some of the blind spots in play scholarship. Because most contemporary scholarship on theories of play approaches it from a position indebted to games and game studies, we often miss opportunities to theorize play more broadly. We fail to appreciate the more robust kernel of cultural signification within it. Within music, play holds many modalities—subtly different expressive palates. We "play" music, yet we also listen to it. When listening to recorded music, the term *playback* is used. And while role-playing game studies has long been aware of how central improvisation is to theater and performance, one must ask if scholars have yet caught on to how central improvisation has been to Black culture, as evident in the scenes of the aforementioned slave songs.

Play has the potential to be repair, but to do so, we must embrace connotations of play that are more clearly connected to the histories and experiences of BIPOC worldwide. These histories are exciting, innovative, and often constructive of affects that encompass more than just the pleasurable. The next chapter focuses on some different examples of play by BIPOC creators to highlight how they bring pain to the fore in our conversations around play.

5
Recentering Blackness in Games and Play

One of the famed voices of Black feminism, bell hooks, begins her essay "Understanding Patriarchy" with an anecdote about a game of marbles. In the story, a four-year-old hooks asks repeatedly to join her brother and father in the game. Her father repeatedly scolds her and tells her "no," until the pressure mounts to a point where her father breaks a board from the door and beats her repeating, "Girls can't do what boys do" (hooks 2010, 2). Of course, the story illustrates the intersectional nature of oppression and how what hooks terms "imperialist white-supremacist capitalist patriarchy" is internalized by Black folk. For the purposes of this book, hooks's story reminds us of exactly the kinds of stories that are lost to the White European definition of play that solely sees it as productive of pleasure. hooks's experience is an earnest retelling of how play can produce affects of trauma, pain, and abuse. In a sense, it is a reminder of how the continued and shared trauma of slavery still haunts the Black community today.

Another example of how a definition of play can embrace its fraught and painful tendencies by recentering the experiences of minoritized people is Jeremy O. Harris's play *Slave Play*. It is a story about a trio of interracial couples who are engaging in sex therapy because the Black partners are no longer attracted to their mates. The play brings race to the forefront of the conversation by foregrounding the discomfort of the White characters in referring to their partners' race. Perhaps even edgier, it has the White characters take the role of the masters or mistresses in BDSM slave play (Harris 2019). In a performance, Harris called for a "Black Out"—only Black-identifying people would attend the play—in order to subvert the affluent White norms of Broadway. He explains to *American Theater*, "For me it was about Black work begetting Black work and Black audiences" (Tran 2019, para. 15). This decision immediately attracted controversy from the conservative theatergoing community. The (presumably White-identifying) *National Review* critic-at-large Kyle Smith quipped, "It would be illegal to refuse to sell tickets based on this or that race" (Smith 2019, para. 2), showing the very discomfort with even discussing the discrimination familiar to all BIPOC people. In the play, themes of role reversal and trauma sharing are imposed upon White theater audiences. Recentering how play intersects with the experience of BIPOC people will rarely produce the same pleasurable affects that games like *Mario Kart* and *Dungeons & Dragons* build into their core gameplay loops.

In Clifford Geertz's (1972) *Deep Play: Notes on the Balinese Cockfight*, he argued that cockfights—no matter how violent and brutal they appeared to outsiders—were a way for the Balinese to understand themselves as a culture. He gestures to the Dutch occupation of 1908 to argue that the violence of colonialism brought the European customs that drove the cockfight—which had previously been situated in the center of all village life—to the margins of society. Similarly, slave games have been forced to the edges of Western society. They only exist now in a handful of history books and through the oral histories shared by the descendants of slavery.

White supremacy conspires to make Whiteness invisible by making Blackness shameful. Kishonna Gray shares how the experience of Black gamers today involves the pain of disclosing their race online. She explains how the question "are you Black?" in a gaming session of *Gears of War* prompted one gamer to downplay their Blackness, shooting back "Why? Are you White?" Things devolved into race-shaming, with taunts of "nigger, nigger" accenting the trauma that the gamer's Blackness was shameful in the eyes of the other players (Gray 2012, 267–8). Approaches to play that read gaming sessions like this as constructive of socialization and learning, while separating the racism occurring in game chat as "not play," are complicit in White supremacy. A reparative approach to play is aggressively anti-racist because it foregrounds how the most painful dynamics of play often exist alongside its most pleasurable aspects.

Let me seed a radical idea: play reduces humans to objects because play is violent. This may seem extreme, but as conversations about race return to the center of political discourse globally, now is the time to rethink the White supremacy of the social and intellectual structures of today's world. Acknowledging the ways that play dehumanizes allows us to recenter and better appreciate games that exist at the margins of Western society. We succumb to colonialism and White supremacy when we assume that play must always produce affects of pleasure. Despite the violence of play, something important might be recovered by a closer analysis of its more dangerous tendencies.

Black Radical Aesthetics

Understanding and appreciating the aesthetics that are borne out of violence, danger, and pain are part of the Black radical tradition. While research in this tradition tends to focus on forms of play that are not gameplay, the multimedia aesthetics that Black designers, composers, writers, and instrumentalists choose speaks to a common tradition. This chapter concludes by offering some ideas about how this tradition theorizes the "break" and offers some examples of Black game designers inhabiting it.

BIPOC game designers have endured abuse, harassment, struggle, and dehumanization as they labor on their excellent games. Here I write about Black game designers because it helps to refine my analysis, draw attention to the tradition of Black radical aesthetics, and highlight how these designers are part of what Hortense Spillers terms a "rupture" in African culture. She writes, "The massive demographic shifts, the violent formation of a modern African consciousness, that takes place on the sub-Saharan Continent during the initiative strikes which open the Atlantic Slave Trade in the fifteenth century of our Christ, interrupted hundreds of tears of black African culture" (Spillers 1987, 68). Contending with the aesthetic, social, and narrative impact of the fissure described by Spillers means sketching the contours of an artistic scene that has endured in spite of hardship.

Fred Moten calls this aesthetic sensibility "the break." For him, it is the essence of the Black radical tradition. It's a recognition that Black radicalism demands holding on to contradictions by embracing both the horror and the hope of Black artistic expression. By way of an example, Moten describes music: Abbey Lincoln's scream in Max Roach's improvisational track "Triptych: Peace/Protest/Prayer" on the album *We Insist!* He writes that Lincoln sounds "troubled by the trace of the performance of which she tells and the performance of which that performance told" (Moten 2003, 22). Is Lincoln in pain or is she exuberant? She's both and neither.

She is the scream; she doesn't own the scream; she's just performing the scream; she is more than a scream. Moten's theorization of Black radical aesthetics remains indebted to W.E.B. Du Bois's double consciousness—where one is always evaluating themselves through the eyes of White society (DuBois 1994, 5). Black artists constantly bring this duality into their work. Their work is radical because *they* are radical. The survival, perseverance, and success of Black people in cultures that have been colonized and defined by White Europeans is itself a radical form of expression.

Perhaps Frantz Fanon wrote it best: "Not only must the black man be black; he must be black in relation to the white man" (Fanon 2008, 82–3). Here, Fanon is referring to the significance of colonization to the construction of Blackness. Blackness—as an identity or as a lived experience—is the result of years, decades, even centuries of subjugation and struggle. Indeed, the brutality and violence of colonization draw the inequity of Blackness into focus and have long been a common point of solidarity among BIPOC people worldwide. My focus on analog game developers of color in this chapter is thus intended to shine a light on a particular history of minoritization. In so doing, I hope to also speak to the unique conditions of Blackness globally.

The Black radical tradition applies to more than just music. In this chapter, I look to games to consider how the Black radical tradition is articulated in design communities today. As I note in the introduction, this is a far more radical intervention than one might at first think. By and large, Black people are largely absent from the publicity and concept art of many early hobby games. I have argued elsewhere that this is because the hobby game scene was mainly the invention of White suburban men, whose networks and aesthetic sensibilities remain dominant (Trammell, forthcoming). The high barrier to entry imbues each analog game from a Black designer with a unique sense of struggle, compromise, and purpose.

In concluding this chapter, I look only to analog game designers because analog games have typically been the black sheep in the field of game studies. Often underrepresented in favor of games that hold a more explicit relationship to technocapital, analog games have been relegated to the margins and footnotes of game studies research for decades (Torner 2018). Yet analog game research speaks most clearly to the club that I identify with. As cofounder and now editor in chief of the journal *Analog Game Studies*, my research frequently focuses on the critical analysis of analog games. In this regard, analog games are my personal "break" from the dominant tradition of game studies. And I delight in the many nuanced ways that Black designers have devised their own aesthetic breaks in their writing.

The aesthetic output of Black game designers *is* multifaceted, complex, and challenging, and that itself is the contradiction of Black radicalism within the analog game scene. While some designers like Chris Spivey and

Julia Bond Ellingboe make explicit overtures toward Black history in their work, others like Eric Lang subvert it by playing with popular culture and remixing historical narratives from the Nordic countries, East Asia, and fantasy worlds. Analog games as a design category traverse many genres, each with a different consumer base, separate distribution network, and even distinct design conventions. Knowing how to speak to, with, and between these different sensibilities speaks to the skill of the designers this book catalogs in the paragraphs that follow.

Analog games are notoriously White in the illustrations that they provide to their players. Consider this brief history. In 1965, Avalon Hill's *General*— wargaming's[1] premier magazine—featured a Black man on the cover. He is the limo driver of Elwood Gardner, one of the company's representatives, and he poses with Elwood and a huge bag of money for a publicity stunt. By 1980, two dark-skinned heroes surround a dragon on the cover of *Dragon*, hobby role-playing's premiere magazine. Two months later, *Dragon* includes a Black high school student in a depiction of a schoolyard. Three months later, a Black student on the cover participates in a food fight with his peers. In 1982, *General* features a rendering of a White Cleopatra on its cover. It wasn't until February 1995 that Dragon would again feature a Black character on its cover—again, a pair of evil Drow (dark/Black) elves, killing an adventurer.

Representation was not much better on the fan circuit. It wasn't until issue number 40 of *Alarums & Excursions*—the main fanzine of *Dungeons & Dragons*—that a Drow elf was featured on the cover. And in the thirty-year time line covered here, there were no more instances of Black people on the covers of any of these three publications. Hobby games, as such, were largely packaged, sold, and presented to their audiences as a space for White cultural production. Even as moments of integration—"Black cool" and multiculturalism—filtered through the American popular consciousness, hobby games insulated themselves from these conversations by marketing to a specific and niche set of consumers.

The tragedy of this story is that Black people have long been active as designers in what I refer to as the analog game scene—a scene composed of the common interests of role-playing game, card game, board game, pervasive game, and live-action role-playing game fans (Torner, Trammell, and Waldron 2014). Take Mike Pondsmith, who was the designer of the 1987 tabletop role-playing game *Cyberpunk 2013*, a game that has now become a franchise, most recently yielding CD Projekt Red's blockbuster *Cyberpunk 2077*. Even though *Cyberpunk 2013* was a cult hit—big enough to influence the development of the AAA video game title forty years later—Pondsmith's race is barely visible in the game itself. In film and theater, the Non-Traditional Casting

Project was only just beginning to advocate for a more inclusive approach to casting roles in popular entertainment media. Pondsmith was publishing for a postal network of predominantly White hobbyists in an era when hobby role-playing games were only available at model train stores.

Pondsmith wasn't alone, and there were many other Black designers in the hobby game scene. Still, I would argue that *Cyberpunk* is a paradigm case in how Black designers are able to subvert the expectations of their readers and play against genre conventions. The tagline of 2019's recently released sourcebook *Cyberpunk Red* reads, "The Roleplaying Game of the Dark Future." The future is dark because Pondsmith articulates a dystopic vision of a future in which corporations run amok, people have found new drugs to tune in and drop out with, and the bustle of urban life is contrasted only against life in the bombed-out wastelands that surround "Night City." The future is also dark because the future is Black. "Night City" is minority White, and the world is, in many ways, imagined from a perspective that takes Black culture for granted and works to make the exotic mundane.

The break lingers in every detail of the world and has even garnered controversy in the game's digital adaptation, *Cyberpunk 2077*. Some critics of Pondsmith's work have suggested that the game furthers racist stereotypes by uncritically presenting BIPOC characters in a gang called "The Animals." Pondsmith's response perfectly captures the essence of Black radical aesthetics: "Who the fuck do YOU think you are to tell ME whether or not MY creation was done right or not?"[2] Pondsmith refuses to be told what Black is, and how Black can identify or disidentify. As a Black author, Pondsmith is vocalizing against the double standard by which his work is being judged. "The Animals" are at once too Black and not Black enough. But Pondsmith inhabits the break. He knows that Black art isn't always legible to White folks, and he eagerly embraces these contradictions in his design.

Eric Lang is one of the most popular board game designers working today. Until 2020, he was the director of game design for Cool Mini or Not, a board game design company that specialized in lightweight, miniature wargames with broad market appeal. Many of Lang's games focus on adapting intellectual property into an exciting board game experience. The list of properties Lang has developed is impressive and includes *Marvel, Game of Thrones, Star Wars, The Godfather,* and *Dilbert.* One of Lang's greatest talents as a designer is being able to imagine how wildly different worlds and settings might be transformed into a board game. Lang is a master of the game remix.

Lang's creative output constantly reimagines and reforms the presumptions that we bring to the game table. His "Mythic Trilogy" of wargames are prime examples of his ability to shift expectations. *Blood Rage* innovates on Norse mythology to imagine a wargame where part of the goal is to kill your own troops and send them to Valhalla. His game *Rising Sun* takes place in feudal Japan, and has a heavy focus on the economic consumption of war. The third game in the trilogy, *Gods of Egypt*, pushes players to contemplate religious dogma. In it, players take on the role of gods in a polytheistic pantheon competing for followers in a world that is turning to monotheism for religion. All of Lang's games in the trilogy allow players to toy with miniatures that represent monsters from the various mythologies.

Black radical aesthetics inhabit Eric Lang's designs too. He subverts conventions of the wargaming genre to bring in more fantastic elements from cultures on the margins. Lang's game designs appropriate and repackage Norse,[3] Japanese, and Egyptian mythologies. He uses these mythologies to recenter BIPOC cultures in a genre that all too frequently fetishizes the history and symbology of White men.[4] Games in this trilogy are also all wargames, a genre that this chapter has already identified as being notoriously White. Rather than adopting them wholesale, Lang appropriates conventions of the wargaming genre and then reskins these games with themes that dive deep into Japanese and Egyptian mythology. In so doing, he opens space for more diverse stories than wargames' celebratory accounts of Confederate general Robert E. Lee and Nazi general Erwin Rommel's military prowess.

Finally, I would be remiss if I didn't end with describing Julia Bond Ellingboe's role-playing game *Steal Away*

Jordan: Stories from America's Peculiar Institution. The game is best described by one of Ellingboe's collaborators, Katherine Castiello Jones in an interview with Ellingboe. Jones writes,

> For those readers who have not yet played the game, *Steal Away Jordan: Stories from America's Peculiar Institution* is a tabletop role-playing game in which players tell the collective stories of enslaved people. Written in the spirit of neo-slave narratives like Margaret Walker's *Jubilee*, Toni Morrison's *Beloved*, and Octavia Butler's *Kindred*, the game is set during the United States' antebellum period. Each session focuses on the struggles of a group of slaves to achieve their secret goals. These range from large goals like killing the overseer, to smaller goals, such as keeping a family member from being sold away, learning to read in secret, or getting a pair of shoes. Players have to work together to achieve their goals, but the game also forces characters to make hard decisions about when to prioritize their own goals over the needs of other characters. Does one make a break for it during a moment of conflict or stand up for another slave as they are interrogated about missing goods? (Jones 2016, para. 2)

Steal Away Jordan retells the story of American slavery. By drawing on the work of Black authors to think through how living through slavery requires managing trauma, scraping by—and even conspiring with one another to achieve freedom, comfort, and even joy—Ellingboe expertly shows how Black radical aesthetics can inform the role-playing game genre.

Often, Ellingboe's critics describe *Steal Away Jordan* pejoratively as not being a game but an educational exercise. Some people were "afraid to play it" (Jones 2016, para. 16). Specifically, critics even related to Ellingboe that they were "afraid of getting it wrong" (Jones 2016, para. 17). In other words, because Ellingboe focuses on the institution of American slavery in her game, the threat of a play experience that touches on trauma was too much for many of the presumably White players who encountered it. "The definition of 'fun' is something that gets policed," Ellingboe recounts, "There is an idea that games have to be fantastical. That a game shouldn't make you think beyond what pleases your character" (Jones 2016, para. 23). But this is life in the hold. We're just holding on to the things that make us Black. The indelible mark that we all carry with us replaces a sense of origin with a common cause and solidarity.

Embracing the painful as well as the pleasurable is what makes Black radical aesthetics so poignant. If Frederick Douglass had omitted Aunt Hester's scream in his *Narrative of the Life of Frederick Douglass*, would it have inspired so many to work toward abolition? Would the flourishes of John Coltrane be so sublime if he didn't improvise both tonal and atonal notes? As Ellingboe so adeptly put it, the Western European canon of play scholars has been mostly concerned with policing the kinds of affect that play is productive of. Sharing the pain of Black fantasy is an important part of the project of Black radical aesthetics. There is a political end to this work, of course. As André Carrington puts it, "Haunting will not go away so long as its conditions of possibility remain intact" (Carrington 2016, 23).

The policing of play that only allows for pleasure allows trauma, death, and pain to haunt Black aesthetics. Although Ellingboe, Lang, and Pondsmith all take different approaches to designing games, the Black radical tradition runs through their work. Within each game lies a desire to surface and make legible the contradictions of White culture. Pondsmith imagines Black futures, Lang subverts genre expectations from within, and Ellingboe simply makes a game of history and encourages us to spend some time inhabiting the traumatic lives of the past. All three, along with so many more Black artists, are haunted. All tell the same story in different ways.

Conclusion: Repairing Play

I came to know with now dismay
That in this world we all must pay
Pay to write, pay to play
Pay to cum, pay to fight
                    —Bad Brains, "Pay to Cum," 1982

Throughout this book, I have alluded to the erasure of Black play. This is the crisis we must address if we are to repair play. The quote above is by the Black DC hardcore band Bad Brains. The excerpt, taken from a short track on their whirlwind eponymous album, laments the cost of creativity, reproduction, and even play for BIPOC people, and in this case, the presumed listeners as well: punks. All the costs that we must pay for—the cost of creativity, the cost of reproduction, the cost of play—are what Stefano Harney and Fred Moten feel render us a fugitive public. They argue that we must find a common cause between the oppressed, BIPOC people, and other fugitive groups on the run from creditors.

For them, the forgiveness of debt is the rehabilitation of capital since it furthers the same destructive logics that have colonized BIPOC people for centuries (Harney and Moten 2013, 64). The problem is that forgiveness maintains the same power relationship that allows the systems of today's bondage, best embodied by debt, to continue.

The question of whether debt must be forgiven is an open one and often takes another name: reparations. In that context, reparations refer to a global coalition of BIPOC people who have had their histories, land, families, and dignity stolen from them by White colonizers. Harney and Moten's case for solidarity in the underground (what they term the *undercommons*), must be contrasted against Ta-Nahesi Coates essay, "The Case for Reparations." Here Coates also writes about debt, and Black farmers in Mississippi who were murdered, harassed, and chased out of the state in antebellum America. Coates explains, "Many of Mississippi's black farmers lived in debt peonage, under the sway of cotton kings who were at once their landlords, their employers, and their primary merchants" (Coates 2014, para. 3). Connecting the dots between this debt and the debt of Black homeowners during the 2009 financial crisis, Coates uses the term "plunder" to describe how the state and other White institutions leveraged debt to exploit Black publics in the United States. In other words, the debt continues to grow. You've got to pay to play.

Repairing play is play that remembers, play that speaks truth to power, and play that is conscientious of its own debts. I started this chapter with some notes on debt and reparations because I am certain that the debts owed by Black people as well as the debts owed to Black people by the appropriative White state are fundamental to understanding a Black phenomenology of play. Remember, Black play is about pain as much as it is about pleasure. The pain that haunts Black communities in the United States, as well as many BIPOC communities globally, is the pain of debt. As long as play is policed by designers and publishers who prefer to publish the pleasurable to the painful, we continue to live in bondage. We remain subordinated by a system of values that continues to neglect, criticize, and deliberately misunderstand Black aesthetics.

The goals of this book are ambitious. It aims to center the experiences of BIPOC people in a theory of play. By writing it, I hope to make scholarship about race more legible to a community that has long focused on a canon of play scholarship invented by a handful of White European men. Even after reading this book, if you continue to find this scholarship illegible, that's okay. Crows speak in jargon because they don't need to be understood. When crows play, are they speaking or are they singing? Beautiful and cacophonous, we reach toward an ideal of play that is only inches away outside of the hold. We lament in sonorous tones how this ideal is somehow always just out of reach.

I began this book by rehearsing some major problems in the canon of play theory. I moved deliberately from Huizinga to Caillois to Piaget to Sutton-Smith because this canon has been built upon a problematic assumption. Most canonical game theory presumes that play is productive of civilization or even consciousness itself. As a game studies scholar, I admire the potency of this argument. However, as a Black man, I remain concerned that this approach to play continues to reify an ideal of civilization that is inherently White supremacist; it defines White European culture as "civilized" and juxtaposes all other cultures against this tautological[1] standard. I maintain that play can still be productive—just as a dream can be productive of ideas—but I argue specifically that play is productive of affect.

Play's connection to affect is intimately linked to the aforementioned discourse of civilization and play. White European definitions of civilization demand that "citizens" act within a particular set of moral standards. Those who don't are exiled, jailed, or shunned for their vulgarity. Huizinga chooses not to write about gambling, while Caillois describes certain forms of vulgar, vertiginous, and unsettling play as "corrupt." Corrupt play is often productive of affects that aren't pleasurable and instead are unsettling and painful. I've argued throughout this book that these affects are key to Black radical aesthetics, and we do ourselves a disservice when they are neglected and isolated from play. To repair play, we must come to understand the painful, the torturous, and challenging aspects of how we play.

Repairing play means rethinking how we understand questions of consent in the games that we play. Canonical approaches to play presume that play is voluntary, specifically because they aim to recover "civilization" from its phenomenology. Repairing play responds by beginning with the assumption that play is not necessarily voluntary and is a potentially hurtful and traumatic activity. But just because play can be hurtful and potentially traumatic, it doesn't follow that the concept itself is problematic. We must tend to play in order to repair it. We must build consent into the games we play and recognize how one person's play is another's prison. Black radical aesthetics don't hit pause before describing the traumatic; instead, they introduce the painful with the thoughtful care it deserves.

If we consider how tending to play and opening up a space for playing with the traumatic might repair it, we must also acknowledge how horrific behaviors like torture are also play. I look to W.E.B. Du Bois to recall the centrality of torture to the Black American experience. Torture evokes a dark fantasy about life in the hold. It reminds us of the objectification that occurs when we are played with. A Black phenomenology of play grounds itself in the affects of torment that play produces, as opposed to the affects of pleasure that the White European canon read as particularly "civilized."

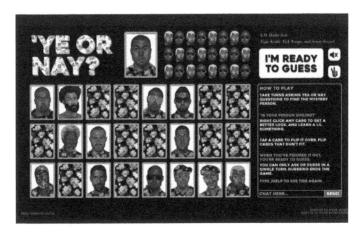

Figure 1
A.M. Darke's *'Ye or Nay?*

Finally, repairing play is an ongoing project. Play cannot be repaired without acknowledging how BIPOC artists work at play through the games they design, songs they sing, and murals they paint. What's more, we repair play when we acknowledge how it drifts above, under, around, and through all artistic media. As it stands, play has been fragmented into aesthetics that have been ghettoized by discipline. A Black phenomenology of play looks to the affects that Black artists aim to conjure to theorize a sense of repair. In other words, there is a common thread that runs between game designer A. M. Darke's brilliant game *'Ye or Nay?*[2] (figure 1)—a clever reskin of the game *Guess Who?* that asks players to identify the correct persona of Kanye West by giving the other player clues and thus contending with their implicit and internal biases—and the

Black performativity of Bad Brains, the first and only Black hardcore band in the Washington, DC, notoriously White hardcore scene. The violent thrash of Black men in DC appropriating and performing music that had been only performed by White men forced people to contend with their biases about what hardcore music was and what it represents. Henry Rollins explains in the documentary *Bad Brains: A Band From D.C.*, "It was the summer of 1979. Word was that there was an all-Black punk rock band in Washington, DC. Never seen one of those before." Repairing play means appreciating how play is polyphonic and can produce affects for both players and listeners across media.

Repairing play is also that which subverts and appropriates the narrative of White play to center BIPOC people and participation. Souvik Mukherjee describes how India's national embrace of the sport cricket is a way of "playing back" by appropriating a British game and embracing it as a symbol of independence and Indian identity (Mukherjee 2017, 4–5). Finding respite from the trauma of colonialism, in other words, and making space for the pleasures of cricket—despite its fraught roots in colonial cultural exchange—is a necessary part of repair. Joy and pleasure are a necessary part of reparations. Mukherjee's ability to find pleasure within cricket despite its dark history runs parallel to the Black phenomenology of play that I have sketched in this book, as it is fundamentally a story of ambivalence that layers pleasure and pain within the singular act of play.

For many, repairing play will undoubtedly be an approach that aims to surface BIPOC narratives that have been rendered invisible by colonialism. This means challenging erasure in all of its many forms. Rhett Loban, a Torres Strait Islander, devised a brilliant modification of the grand strategy title *Europa Universalis IV*—a game that simulates war, exploitation, and colonization—called "Indigenous People of Oceania." The modification is simulationist and succeeds in better reflecting the culture of the indigenous oceanic peoples. Yet despite this success, Loban laments the structural limitations he ran into during the modding process. Better representing indigenous people in *Europa Universalis IV* meant buying into the agonist and colonial context of the game itself and making them their own nation-states (Loban and Apperley 2019, 94–5). Here the act of repair became also an act of assimilation, interpolating the narrative of war, power, exploitation, and colonization onto the islanders represented in Loban's modification.

Perfection cannot be a virtue as we strive to repair play. Moving forward means recognizing that perfection itself is a European value that churns and erodes our wayward souls. Perfection and perfectionism are internalized forms of discipline that elevate purity as an aesthetic value. Repairing play is aligned with the messy imperfect and everyday values that are at ease with the postindustrial landscapes we inhabit where things are often imperfect and broken, and people are just "making do." For this reason, "Indigenous People of Oceania," cricket, Darke, and Bad Brains all repair play. This coalition is exemplified by a broad and aesthetically diverse set of radical projects, all of which resist facile readings that would undermine their critical strengths for the pleasurable capture of perfection.

The colonial project of play that aligns its potential with civilization is in its sunset years. Repairing play must tend not only to the legacy of civilizing play. It must tend toward a speculative Black future where we play together in a web of mutual aid, supporting one another through both challenging and joyful times. I chose the adverb "repairing" to modify play not only because it is part of the etymology of "reparations." I also selected it because I see repair too as a form of play that is able to address the production of painful affects that it produces. In so doing, repair might heal the damage that colonialism has wrought.

In the introduction to this book, I drew attention to the enigmatic Black children's game, "Hide the Switch." Let us end with it, too, as it shows how repairing play helps to make sense of play that would have been previously been read as barbaric. Defining this game as not play at all would contribute to Black erasure. "Hide the Switch" forces game scholars to reconsider what and who has been left out of spaces that curate games and play. It shows how the traumatic memory of Black people descended from slaves cannot be read as play, as it is often theorized. Therefore, such trauma cannot easily fit into White memory institutions like museums that merely celebrate play. We prefer our games to be safe and consensual, but as a result, we have forgotten that games themselves are not always safe and consensual. In fact, it is a privileged position that assumes this because play is often violent. Play forces us to contend with the truth that we must always negotiate our own experience with that of others. This is what the brutality of "Hide the Switch" reveals. It shows how torture is as mundane a phenomenon as play and that all are capable of its cruel pleasures. To forget this is to aestheticize the experience of play and to resign ourselves to the cultural norms of White supremacy.

Notes

Introduction

1. Although this work engages in a deep conversation about the legacies of colonialism and the slave trade, it is not related to the politics of the American Descendants of Slavery (ADOS) movement. Proponents of ADOS differentiate between Black Americans descended from slaves and Black Americans who do not share this history for largely political ends (state-sanctioned reparations, for instance). I keep my focus on the tragic impacts of colonialism specifically because they are the common ground that unite all BIPOC people historically, economically, and even representationally in solidarity against common forms of oppression. So even though this book considers the history of slavery in North America in some detail, it does so only to make one part of a larger point about the deep and common history of torture and abuse devised by imperialist and colonialist efforts.

2. Let me go a little deeper. In this book, I often toggle between Black and BIPOC. My use of these terms is deliberate in the text and intended to hail the respective populations noted. In other words, when I use the word *Black*, I use it to refer to Black Americans, and when I use the term *BIPOC*, it connotes all BIPOC globally, including Black Americans. I vary my usage because this book draws on American studies, specifically that which relates to the Black American experience, in order to make a broader argument about the invisibility of BIPOC trauma, pain, and feeling in White spaces of play. And

while I recognize that the Black American experience is not universal, it is just one voice in the greater BIPOC chorus, it is my hope that the shared sense of suffering wrought from these experiences will act as a tonic by grounding this theory of play in something common.

3. A careful reader might note that Huizinga does discuss games of chance in his writing—for example, he discusses the use of dice games in the Indian epic *The Mahabharata*. In these instances, however, Huizinga fails to relate how gambling might produce socioeconomic disparity.

4. It is worth noting here that Rosa Eidepes's historical work reveals a critique of Roger Caillois by Theodore Adorno for holding "cryptofascist tendencies." Adorno contended that Caillois uncritically defaulted to a sublime notion of the "natural order" (Eidepes 2014, 9). Although I agree with this critique, I take an ambivalent stance toward the political beliefs of Caillois and other play scholars described in this book. I believe that the theorizing of play done by these figures is problematic only insofar as they adopt a moral stance toward the concept. By recentering the ways that play can be torturous, "corrupt," or painful, we curb fascist, racist, and sexist tendencies that set White culture or "civilization" against a "barbaric" natural order.

5. Constructivists argue that knowledge is constructed through action and experience. Piaget and Vygotsky argue that through play in particular people learn fundamentals, such as language. While for Piaget this play was more individual and for Vygotsky this play was more interpersonal, the overall educational theory of constructivism argues that informal and playful practices are often the foundation upon which institutional and formal structures of education—school for example—are built.

6. Mahli-Ann Rakkomkaew Butt and Thomas Apperley have argued that approaches to inclusivity in gaming often involve assimilation into a problematic heteronormative male status quo. I would add that the assimilative norms of inclusivity frequently suggest that Black folks should assimilate to a White supremacist status quo as well (Butt and Apperley 2018, 39).

7. I use this term in the valence intended by my colleague Roderic Crooks who suggests that it makes visible the power relationships of minority people as opposed to their demography (Crooks 2019, 119).

8. Russworm makes this point well in her book that explains how the history of games is itself a White supremacist enterprise (or in her words "White. White. White.") The stories of BIPOC people, developers, and designers are often occluded in historical projects that center White designers and developers of games (Russworm 2019).

Chapter 1

1. This statement was recorded here: https://www.laughingplace.com /w/news/2019/04/30/floyd-norman-defends-dumbo-crow-scene-amid -rumors-potential-censorship/

2. Huizinga argued that without play, we would lack the fundamental ingredients for myth and ritual. Without these approaches to communication, there would be no institutions of "civilized" life. He wrote, "Archaic society, we would say, plays as the child or animal plays. Such playing contains at the outset all the elements proper to play: order, tension, movement, change, solemnity, rhythm, rapture. Only in a later phase of society is play associated with the idea of something to be expressed in and by it, namely, what we would call 'life' or 'nature.' Then, what was wordless play assumes poetic form. In the form and function of play, itself and independent entity that is senseless and irrational, man's consciousness that he is imbedded in a sacred order of things finds its first, highest, and holiest expression. Gradually the significance of a sacred act permeates the playing. Ritual grafts itself upon it; but the primary thing is and remains play" (Huizinga 1980, 17–8).

3. Piaget writes, "The phenomenon of 'pre-exercise,' which K. Groos considered the characteristic of all play, can only be explained by the biological process according to which every organ develops through use" (1962, 87).

4. To Piaget, play is an essential part of the meaning-making process. Play, as an act, spoke to the assimilative potential of the mind. It

opposed the associative qualities of thought, which Piaget considered mere imitation. The moment of play/assimilation, for Piaget, is a primal drive to power: "Play, on the contrary [to imitation], proceeds by relaxation of the effort at adaptation and by maintenance or exercise of activities for the mere pleasure of mastering them and acquiring thereby a feeling of virtuosity or power" (Piaget 1962, 89).

5. Piaget feels that the play of magic serves as an early stage of meaning-making for children. However, argues that they quickly grow out of it when they are able to arrive at "objective notions" (Piaget 1962, 261). But what of cultures and people for whom "magic" is regularly still practiced through ritual? I conjecture that Piaget would either dismiss these rituals as superstition and question whether the people practicing truly "believe" in the magic or simply see these spiritual beliefs as childish.

6. Caillois (2001) writes, "Just as the principle of *agôn* (competition) is abruptly destroyed by vertigo, *alea* (chance) is similarly destroyed [by mimicry] and there is no longer any game, properly speaking." (73)

7. Spariousu (1989) explains, "Pre-rational thought generally conceives of play as a manifestation of power in its 'natural,' unashamed, unmediated form, ranging from the sheer delight of emotional release to raw and arbitrary violence. Power can be experienced both as ecstatic, exuberant, and violent play and as a pleasurable welling up and gushing forth of strong emotion. Rational thought, in contrast, generally separates play from both unmediated or 'innocent' power and raw violence. Indeed, it sees play as a form of mediation between what it now represses as the 'irrational' (the chaotic conflict of physical forces, the disorderly eruption of violent emotion, the unashamed gratification of the physical senses, etc.) and controlling Reason, or the universal Will to Order" (Spariousu, 12).

Chapter 2

1. Akil explains that the post was later reprinted by a number of news outlets, including "Kotaku, Quartz, Mic, Huffington Post, and POPSUGAR. Various news sites, such as Vox, NPR, *USA Today*, VIBE,

Slate, the Mary Sue, and a few others also referenced the piece. It was even mentioned in an episode of *The Young Turks.*"

2. The murder has not stopped. Famously the killing of George Flyod and Breona Taylor remind us today of Akil's point. Being Black in the United States means that you are subject to a separate set of laws and that your life is seen as less important than that of your White neighbors by law enforcement.

3. For Ahmed, happy objects are characterized less by whether they themselves are "happy" but rather a perceived happiness that they might one day produce. For example, a new car might be a happy object even if the loan payments that accompany the car produce a good deal of sorrow. Succinctly, happy objects are productive of both pleasurable and painful affects specifically because they promise happiness.

4. As Anne Allison (2009) explains, "As it is true everywhere around the world today, a more flexible (*ryudoka*) economy is emerging: one based ever more on service rather than manufacturing, and on the irregular pulsations of a market driven by information, communication and speculation" (90). This shift toward a service economy is relevant to Hardt's (1999) concept of affective labor—the dimension of labor concerned with human contact and interaction (95). Affective labor is undercompensated in our society. As Bernard Steigler has noted, we have not yet produced systems of care to match the explosive growth of the new technologically networked society (Crogan 2010, 166).

Chapter 3

1. This practice is also termed "rules lawyering." Steven Dashiell (2017) goes to great lengths to describe the perks of rules lawyering—namely, the social capital this knowledge provides players who police the rules.

2. In his reading of Huizinga, play theorist Peter McDonald describes the figure of the spoilsport as being key to understanding the free and liberating dimensions that Huizinga wanted to theorize within play.

For play to be truly liberating, in Huizinga's philosophy, one must have the freedom to transgress the rules and spoil a game (McDonald 2019, 257).

Chapter 4

1. No apparent relationship to W.E.B.

2. As noted in the introduction, "dark play" and the often-related BDSM play have been a fascination of both game studies scholars and some contemporary scholars of play. These accounts of play generally share the common premise that play is voluntary and consensual. As Jaakko Stenros observes, the very category of "dark play" is predicated on the premise that most play is "positive" (Stenros 2019, 13). My account of play aims to deepen this work by suggesting that play is rarely voluntary. For more on this, see *The Dark Side of Gameplay* (Mortensen, Linderoth, and Brown 2018) and *Transgression in Games and Play* (Jørgensen and Karlsen 2018).

Chapter 5

1. Wargames are typically games played with cardboard chits or miniatures on a large hexagonal grid overlayed atop a map. They were the dominant hobby game scene in the 1960s, and Avalon Hill was the main publisher of wargames at the time. *Risk* and *Diplomacy* are two of the more famous wargames published by Avalon Hill.

2. A good summary of the exchange is available here: https://www .videogameschronicle.com/news/cyberpunk-creator-responds-to-2077 -criticism-who-do-you-think-you-are/.

3. I do not think Lang is making a statement about race and BIPOC culture in the game *Blood Rage*. Instead, I think Lang was using the rich mythology of Nordic culture to design a game that would make his design work legible to a community of largely White hobbyists.

4. I recount a short history of Avalon Hill and TSR Hobbies' magazine covers earlier in this chapter to help make this point. Another excellent example of a typical attitude toward representing BIPOC

people in wargames is the atrociously titled book by Phil Eklund in his simulationist game Pax Parmir, *In Defense of British Colonialism*. Pax Parmir is about indigenous communities being played against one another by colonial rule. Here Eklund writes, "British rule was more stable than the weak, corrupt, and capricious regimes they replaced. Both India and Afghanistan had suffered from centuries of battles between petty warlords. But in India, British rule brought a century of peace, marred only by the localized 1857 Indian Mutiny. Upon Indian independence in 1947, the end of Pax Britannica immediately sparked the Tamil separatist movement, as well as an endless series of Indo-Pakistani wars and conflicts. Since both countries now have the bomb, the next war could be nuclear, with dire consequences for the world." Eklund's description highlights the degree to which some designers still view the culture of BIPOC people as barbaric and in so doing continue to frame Western European culture as that which is "civilized," thus presuming that all others are barbaric. You can find this excerpt from the Pax Parmir rulebook here: https://playthesethings.files.wordpress.com/2018/11/pax_pamir_excerpt.pdf.

Conclusion

1. That is, White European culture is "civilized" because "civilization" is defined by a set of White European standards, not according to any objective criteria.

2. https://files.curiobot.com/theotherlab/yeornay/v0/10/12/.

References

Ahmed, Sara. 2004. "Affective Economies." *Social Text* 22, no. 2: 117–39.

Ahmed, Sara. 2006. "Orientations: Toward a Queer Phenomenology." *GLQ: A Journal of Lesbian and Gay Studies* 12, no. 4: 543–74.

Akil, Omari. 2016. "Warning: Pokémon GO Is a Death Sentence If You Are a Black Man. *Medium.*" https://medium.com/dayone-a-new -perspective/warning-pokemon-go-is-a-death-sentence-if-you-are-a -black-man-acacb4bdae7f.

Allison, Anne. 2009. "The Cool Brand, Affective Activism and Japanese Youth." *Theory, Culture & Society* 26, no. 2–3: 89–111.

Anable, Aubrey. 2018. *Playing with Feelings: Video Games and Affect.* Minneapolis: University of Minnesota Press.

Aristotle. 1944. *Politics.* Translated by Harris Rackham. Cambridge, MA: Harvard University Press.

Bowman, Sarah Lynne. 2010. *The Functions of Role-Playing Games: How Participants Create Community, Solve Problems, and Explore Identity.* Durham, NC: McFarland.

Brennan, Theresa. 2004. *The Transmission of Affect.* Ithaca, NY: Cornell University Press.

Butler, Judith. 1990. *Gender Trouble: Feminism and the Subversion of Identity.* New York: Routledge.

Butt, Mahli-Ann Rakkomkaew, and Thomas Apperley. 2018. "'Shut Up and Play': Vivian James and the Presence of Women in Gaming Cultures." In *Decolonizing the Digital: Technology as Cultural Practice*, edited by Josh Harle, Angie Abdille, and Andrew Newman, 39–47. Sydney: Tactical Space Lab. http://ojs.decolonising.digital/index.php/decolonising_digital/article/view/ShutUpAndPlay.

Caillois, Roger. 2001. *Man, Play and Games*. Urbana: University of Illinois Press.

Carrington, André. 2016. *Speculative Blackness: The Future of Race in Science Fiction*. Minneapolis: University of Minnesota Press.

Coates, Ta-Nehisi. 2014. "The Case for Reparations." *Atlantic*, June 2014. https://www.theatlantic.com/magazine/archive/2014/06/the-case-for-reparations/361631/.

Crogan, Patrick. 2010. *Gameplay Mode: War, Simulation, and Technoculture*. Minneapolis: University of Minnesota Press.

Crooks, Roderic. 2019. "Times Thirty: Access, Maintenance, and Justice." *Science, Technology, & Human Values* 44, no. 1: 118–242. https://doi.org/10.1177/0162243918783053.

Cvetkovich, Ann. 2012. *Depression: A Public Feeling*. Durham, NC: Duke University Press.

Dashiell, Steven. 2017. "Rules Lawyering as Symbolic and Linguistic Capital." *Analog Game Studies* 4, no. 5. https://analoggamestudies.org/2017/11/rules-lawyering-as-symbolic-and-linguistic-capital/.

Douglass, Frederick. 1845. *Narrative of the Life of Frederick Douglass, an American Slave*. Boston: The Anti-Slavery Office.

Du Bois, Page. 2007. "Torture and Truth." In *The Phenomenon of Torture: Readings and Commentary*, edited by William Schulz, 13–15. Philadelphia: University of Pennsylvania Press.

Du Bois, W.E.B. 1994. *The Souls of Black Folk*. Mineola, NY: Dover Publications.

Duncan, Margaret Carlisle. 1988. "Play Discourse and the Rhetorical Turn: A Semiological Analysis of *Homo Ludens*." *Play & Culture* 1: 28–42.

Eidepes, Rosa. 2014. "Roger Caillois' Biology of Myth and the Myth of Biology." *Anthropology & Materialism* 2. https://doi.org/10.4000/am.84.

Fanon, Frantz. 2008. *Black Skin, White Masks*. London: Pluto Books.

Fickle, Tara. 2019. *The Race Card: From Gaming Technologies to Model Minorities*. New York: NYU Press.

Fine, Gary Alan. 2002. *Shared Fantasy: Role-Playing Games as Social Worlds*. Chicago: Univesity of Chicago Press.

Foucault, Michel. 1977. *Discipline and Punish: The Birth of the Prison*. New York: Random House.

Foucault, Michel. 1978. *The History of Sexuality*. New York: Random House.

Fuchs, Mathias. 2014. "Ludoarcheology." *Games & Culture* 9, no. 6: 528–38.

Geertz, Clifford. 1972. "Deep Play: Notes on the Balinese Cockfight." *Daedalus* 101, no. 1: 1–37.

Gray, Kishonna L. 2012. "Deviant Bodies, Stigmatized Identities, and Racist Acts: Examining the Experiences of African-American Gamers in Xbox Live." *New Review of Hypermedia and Multimedia* 18, no 4: 261–276.

Gray, Kishonna L. 2020. *Intersectional Tech: Black Users and Digital Gaming*. Baton Rouge: LSU Press.

Hardt, Michael. 1999. "Affective Labor." *Boundary 2* 26, no. 2: 89–100.

Harney, Stefano, and Fred Moten. 2013. *The Undercommons: Fugitive Planning & Black Study*. New York: Autonomedia.

Harris, Jeremy O. 2019. *Slave Play*. New York: Theater Communications Group.

Harviainen, T. 2011. "Sadomasochist Role-Playing as Live-Action Role-Playing: A Trait-Descriptive Analysis." *International Journal of Role-Playing* 2. http://ijrp.subcultures.nl.

Heinrich, Bernard, and Rachel Smolker. 1998. "Play in Common Ravens (*Corvus corax*)." In *Animal Play*, edited by Marc Bekoff and John A. Byers, 27–44. Cambridge: Cambridge University Press.

Hofer, Margaret. *The Games We Played: The Golden Age of Board and Tabletop Games*. New York: Princeton Architectural Press.

hooks, bell. 2010. *Understanding Patriarchy*. Louisville, KY: Louisville Anarchist Federation Federation. https://imaginenoborders.org/pdf/zines/UnderstandingPatriarchy.pdf.

Huizinga, Johan. 1980. *Homo Ludens: A Study of the Play-element in Culture*. New York: Routledge.

Jones, Katherine Castiello. 2016. "'A Lonely Place': An Interview with Julia Bond Ellingboe." *Analog Game Studies* 3, no. 1. https://analoggamestudies.org/tag/julia-ellingboe/.

Jørgensen, Kristine and Faltin Karlsen, eds. 2019. *Transgression in Games and Play*. Cambridge, MA: MIT Press.

Juul, Jesper. 2005. *Half-Real: Video Games Between Real Rules and Fictional Worlds*. Cambridge, MA: MIT Press.

King, Wilma. 2011. *Stolen Childhood: Slave Youth in Nineteenth-Century America*. Bloomington: Indiana University Press.

Leonard, David J. 2004. "High Tech Blackface: Race, Sports, Video Games and Becoming the Other." *Intelligent Agent* 4, no 4. http://www.intelligentagent.com/archive/Vol4_No4_gaming_leonard.htm.

Leonard, David J. 2006. "Not a Hater, Just Keepin' It Real: The Importance of Race- and Gender-Based Game Studies." *Games and Culture* 1, no. 1: 83–88.

Loban, Rhett, and Tom Apperley. 2019. "Eurocentric Values at Play: Modding the Colonial from an Indigenous Perspective." In *Video Games and the Global South*, edited by Phillip Penix-Tadsen, 87–100. Pittsburgh, PA: ETC Press.

Malkowski, Jennifer, and TreaAndrea M. Russworm. 2017. "Introduction: Identity, Representation, and Video Game Studies." In *Gaming Representation: Race, Gender, and Sexuality in Video Games*, edited by

Jennifer Malkowski and TreaAndrea M. Russworm, 1–18. Indianapolis: Indiana University Press.

McDonald, Peter. 2019. *"Homo Ludens*: A Renewed Reading." *American Journal of Play* 11, no. 2: 247–267.

Mortensen, Torill Elvira, Jonas Linderoth, and Ashley ML Brown, eds. 2015. *The Dark Side of Game Play: Controversial Issues in Playful Environments*. Routledge Advances in Game Studies. New York: Routledge.

Moten, Fred. 2003. *In the Break: The Aesthetics of the Black Radical Tradition*. Minneapolis: University of Minnesota Press.

Mukherjee, Souvik. 2017. *Video Games and Postcolonialism: Empire Plays Back*. New York: Palgrave Macmillan.

Mukherjee, Souvik. 2018. "Playing Subaltern: Video Games and Post-colonialism." *Games and Culture* 13, no. 5: 504–520.

Muñoz, José Esteban. 1999. *Disidentifications: Queers of Color and the Performance of Politics*. Minneapolis: University of Minnesota Press.

Muñoz, José Esteban. 2006. "Feeling Brown, Feeling Down: Latina Affect, the Performativity of Race, and the Depressive Position." *Signs* 31, no. 3: 675–688.

Murray, Soraya. 2018. "The Work of Postcolonial Game Studies in the Play of Culture." *Open Library of Humanities* 4, no. 1: 1–25. https://doi.org/10.16995/olh.285.

Nakamura, Lisa. 2005. "Race In/For Cyberspace: Identity Tourism and Racial Passing on the Internet." *Work and Days* 13. https://smg.media.mit.edu/library/nakamura1995.html.

Piaget, Jean. 1962. *Play, Dreams and Imitation in Childhood*. New York: W. W. Norton & Company.

Russworm, TreaAndrea M. 2019. "Video Game History and the Fact of Blackness." *ROMchip* 1, no. 1. https://romchip.org/index.php/romchip-journal/article/view/85.

Russworm, TreaAndrea M., and Samantha Blackmon. 2020. "Replaying Video Game History as a Mixtape of Black Feminist Thought."

Feminist Media Histories 6, no.1: 93–118. https://doi.org/10.1525/fmh .2020.6.1.93.

Salen, Katie, and Eric Zimmerman. 2003. *Rules of Play: Game Design Fundamentals*. Cambridge, MA: MIT Press.

Sawyer, Ben, and P. Smith. 2008. "Serious Games Taxonomy." Paper presented at the Serious Games Summit at the Game Developers Conference, San Francisco, CA, USA, February 18–22.

Schultz, William F. 2007. *The Phenomenon of Torture: Readings and Commentary*. Philadelphia: University of Pennsylvania Press.

Sicart, Miguel. 2014. *Play Matters*. Cambridge, MA: MIT Press.

Smith, Kyle. 2019. "Broadway Blackout." *National Review*, September 18. https://www.nationalreview.com/corner/broadway-blackout/.

Spariosu, Mihai. 1989. *Dionysus Reborn: Play and the Aesthetic Dimension in Modern Philosophical and Scientific Discourse*. Ithaca, NY: Cornell University Press.

Spillers, Hortense. 1987. "Mama's Baby, Papa's Maybe: An American Grammar Book." *Diacritics* 17, no. 2. https://www.jstor.org/stable /464747.

Stenros, Jaakko, and Sarah Lynne Bowman. 2018. "Transgressive Role-Play." In *Role-Playing Game Studies: Transmedia Foundations*, edited by José Zagal and Sebastian Deterding, 411–424. New York: Routledge.

Stenros, Jaakko. 2019. "Guided by Transgressions: Defying Norms as an Integral Part of Play." In *Transgression in Games and Play*, edited by Kristine Jørgensen and Faltin Karlsen, 13–26. Cambridge, MA: MIT Press.

Stoever, Jennifer. 2016. *The Sonic Color Line: Race and the Cultural Politics of Listening*. New York: NYU Press.

Sutton-Smith, Brian. 1997. *The Ambiguity of Play*. Cambridge, MA: Harvard University Press.

Torner, Evan, Aaron Trammell, and Emma Leigh Waldron. 2014. "Reinventing Analog Game Studies." *Analog Game Studies* 1, no. 1. https://analoggamestudies.org/2014/08/reinventing-analog-game-studies/.

Torner, Evan. 2018. "Just (The Institution of Computer) Game Studies." *Analog Game Studies* 5, no. 2. https://analoggamestudies.org/2018/06/just-the-institution-of-computer-game-studies/.

Trammell, Aaron. Forthcoming. *Geek Culture: A History of Hobby Games, Race, and the Privilege of Play.* Unpublished Manuscript. New York: NYU Press.

Tran, Diep. 2019. "How 'Slave Play' Got 800 Black People to the Theater." *American Theater*, September 23. https://www.americantheatre.org/2019/09/23/how-slave-play-got-800-black-people-to-the-theatre/.

Vossen, Emma. 2018. "The Magic Circle and Consent in Gaming Practices." In *Feminism in Play*, edited by Kishonna Gray, Gerald Voorhees, and Emma Vossen, 205–220. Cham, Switzerland: Palgrave Macmillan.

Vygotsky, Lev. (1966) 2015. "Igra I Ee Rol v Umstvennom Razvitii Rebenka [Play and Its Role in the Mental Development of the Child]." *Voprosy psihologii* [*Problems of Psychology*] 12, no. 6: 62–76.

Weiss, Margot. 2011. *Circuits of Pleasure: BDSM and the Circuits of Sexuality.* Durham, NC: Duke University Press.

Wilderson III, Frank B. 2020. *Afropessimism.* New York: Liveright.

Zimmerman, Eric. 2012. "Jerked Around by the Magic Circle—Clearing the Air Ten Years Later." *Gamasutra*, February 7. https://www.gamasutra.com/view/feature/135063/jerked_around_by_the_magic_circle_.php.

Index